How Science Works

Also available from Continuum

Reflective Teaching of Science 11-18, John Parkinson
Getting the Buggers into Science, Christine Farmery
100 Ideas for Teaching Science, Sharon Archer

How Science Works

Teaching and Learning in the Science Classroom

James D. Williams

continuum

Continuum International Publishing Group

The Tower Building   80 Maiden Lane
11 York Road   Suite 704
London SE1 7NX   New York, NY 10038

www.continuumbooks.com

British Library Cataloguing-in-Publication Data
A catalogue record for this book is available from the British Library.

ISBN: 978-1-4411-4707-3 (paperback)
       978-1-4411-3642-8 (hardcover)

Library of Congress Cataloging-in-Publication Data
Williams, James D. (James Dale), 1949-
How science works : teaching and learning in the science classroom /
    James D. Williams.
      p. cm.
    Includes index.
    ISBN: 978-1-4411-4707-3 (pbk.)
    ISBN: 978-1-4411-3642-8 (hardcover)
    1. Science–Study and teaching–Philosophy. 2. Inquiry-based learning.
    I. Title.
    Q181.W726 2011
    507.1–dc22
                                                    2010029090

Typeset by Newgen Imaging Systems Pvt Ltd, Chennai, India
Printed and bound in India

Contents

viii Contents

Introduction

The recent shift from teaching the facts of science to the process of science, or How Science Works, represents the most major and fundamental reform of science teaching since the introduction of science as a core subject at the inception of the national curriculum in 1988. The aim of science education has sometimes been unclear. Are we laying the foundation of a scientific workforce to ensure our competitive edge in world economics? Or are we simply ensuring that past, current and future generations of children are scientifically literate and able to cope in an increasingly complex and technological society? Perhaps the aim of a good science education is to enable young people to engage in debate that may affect their lives – should human cloning be allowed? Is it ethical to use stem cells for the development of medical treatments? Perhaps all of these things are vital in a good science education – a grounding in basic facts, a consideration of the moral and ethical dimensions of science, the ability to understand arguments between competing standpoints.

This book explores the new approach to science, made statutory with the new programmes of study. It looks at aspects of the history and philosophy of science, argumentation and the language of science and provides a background for science teachers and those involved in science education which is often missing from their own education in science. A study of the history and philosophy of science is not a compulsory or common component of a standard undergraduate degree. Yet dealing with How Science Works requires a basic understanding of these aspects of the discipline. The chapter headings are self-explanatory and, to a large extent, stand alone. The intention is that the book should be a handy reference for key aspects of How Science Works rather than a study text which needs to be read from cover to cover in a particular order.

The book begins with a chapter on understanding the nature of science. It examines what we mean by 'the nature of science' and how this relates to the new approach to teaching science in schools. Research shows that science teachers' understanding of the nature of science is not well developed. This is also an issue for professional scientists whose understanding of their discipline tends to focus only on the practical aspects of their day-to-day work. They take little time to consider the roots and development of their discipline and how this, in effect, defines the discipline.

Chapter 2 provides a brief history of science from its earliest days through the scientific revolution and on to more recent major discoveries in science such as Darwin and Wallace's theory of evolution by means of natural selection. In part this chapter begins to define what makes science 'science' a theme that will be developed in Chapter 3.

Chapter 3 looks at aspects of the philosophy of science including Popper's falsification ideas and Kuhn's scientific paradigms. This chapter engages with the basic question that any discipline must answer – in this case what makes science, 'science'. The question may appear to have an obvious answer, but it is a question that has taxed philosophers and scientists for centuries. Gaining an understanding of how we define our discipline helps us, and ultimately our pupils, to distinguish real science, for example evolution or astronomy from pseudoscience, creationism or astrology. What this chapter does not do is settle the philosophical debates about the meaning of science, but it does offer a definition that suffices for school science and enables pupils to grasp the characteristics of a scientific approach from an approach that may appear scientific but which is in fact pseudoscientific. This in itself will be a major boost to scientific literacy if that one aspect of How Science Works alone is successful.

Chapter 4 considers the language of science, but not just the scientific terminology which has its roots in Latin and Greek – or the roots, suffixes and prefixes of scientific words which, if taught and understood, will demystify much of science. It considers some of the key terminology of science such as what we mean by the terms law, fact, theory and hypothesis. Many of these words (in common with many science words) will have a common or vernacular meaning as well as a strict scientific meaning. Teaching about How Science Works should draw this distinction to the attention of our pupils. I would also go so far as to suggest that key terminology should, for the sake of school science, be modified slightly to make the distinction between the vernacular use of certain words and scientific use. By discussing and talking about scientific theories or scientific hypotheses or scientific facts we will be able to avoid dismissive phrases such as 'it's just a theory' used by some who misunderstand what a scientific theory is and how in science the theory is the accepted explanation for natural phenomena and not just an idea or guess that is waiting for evidence or proof. Through an exploration of the various approaches taken to the development of theories and understanding what the status of facts, theories, laws and hypotheses is in addressing 'the scientific method', this chapter links back to Chapter 1 and the idea of 'The Nature of Science'.

Questions in science are, some would say, the heart of science. It is by asking questions that science, in part, proceeds. Finding answers and explanations is the core of scientific investigation. Chapter 5 discovers what the difference is between a scientific and a non-scientific question. It describes how we can help pupils formulate scientific questions and how to recognize non-scientific questions.

Having considered the nature of science, what makes science 'science', defined some of the key terminology and how we construct scientific questions, Chapter 6 proposes a model for How Science Works. One aspect of the introduction of How Science Works to the new science education curriculum was the lack of a coherent or accepted model for How Science Works. This model integrates experimentation and investigation (what many pupils and science teachers see as the core of science teaching and learning) with aspects not always considered fully, even during the professional and higher education of scientists and science teachers alike – argumentation and the history and philosophy of science. The chapter reflects on previous chapters and integrates and interrelates these ideas.

Chapter 7 discusses the importance of argumentation in science. Although talking in science lessons and talking about science in lessons is common it is often not directed and focused. In this chapter we will look at how we talk about science in the classroom, what the nature of science classroom discourse is, as well as considering how scientists construct arguments. We will consider what we mean by argumentation and how argumentation can be an effective tool in learning and understanding scientific principles and concepts.

The new programmes of study for science at key stages 3 and 4 have brought to the fore aspects of moral and ethical issues in science. While science teachers have traditionally covered moral and ethical issues in science lessons, it has never been as explicit as it is currently and it has never been systematically tackled as an approach to teaching science. Science cannot be without morals and ethics – in today's society too many health issues, medical developments and scientific achievements impact on the lives of people for us to ignore the moral and ethical considerations of what scientists do and achieve. This is an important dimension of How Science Works. Chapter 8 will look at how science copes and deals with moral and ethical issues using examples of past issues (e.g. cloning, embryo design/manipulation, production of weapons of mass destruction) and discusses how these issues can be addressed in science lessons.

Investigation and Experimentation in science has, until now, been the main approach to the teaching of science used by countless science teachers and educators. Recently there have been reports that practical science work in schools has declined and is harming science education. It would be silly to think about teaching science without a practical element since the skills developed and the practical illustration of key concepts are fundamental to engaging young people with the discipline and encouraging them to take further, higher study of science. Chapter 9 looks at the area that teachers are most familiar with and gets behind the terminology that is now present in the GCSE and As/A specifications, for example, precision, accuracy, validity, reliability etc.

Whatever approach is taken to do the 'business' of science, ultimately that science has to be communicated. Chapter 10 looks at the various ways in which science is communicated from academic and technical writing to professional writing and conference presentations down to using newspapers in communicating ideas and how science can be badly communicated.

Chapter 11 finally tries to describe how scientists work, rather than how science works. How scientists really work is different from our ideas of the scientific method, whatever that may or may not be. In this chapter the work of contemporary and historical figures in science is considered to exemplify the approach of different types of scientists to their work and how this relates to the model of HSW outlined in Chapter 4.

What this book cannot do is deliver a teaching scheme for how science works. Its intention is that science teachers gain a broader understanding of the nature of science, a greater understanding of their discipline from its foundations to the present day. It may well pose questions to which there is no one correct or simple answer. Science, unlike how many perceive it, is not about right and wrong, truth or falsehood; it often does not deliver definitive answers.

Science is a growing developing and evolving discipline that proceeds, often, in fits and starts. The next scientific revolution may just be around the corner. The next big idea and theory to explain what is a current mystery – such as the origin of life or the origin of our universe may be revealed in the next 10, 20, 50 or 100 years. That's the excitement of science, not what we know, but what we do not yet know, or more importantly, understand. How Science Works should equip all of our students with the skills to read about scientific ideas and discoveries and, rather than proclaim ignorance, be equipped to investigate further and understand the implications of what they are reading. For those who wish to study science at a higher level, How Science Works should equip them with critical thinking skills and a basic knowledge of scientific concepts, facts and processes which allows them to develop their knowledge and understanding. Finally How Science Works should embed in the students a sense of knowing about the discipline of science, what science is and what it is not, what it can and cannot do.

James Williams
March 2010

1 Understanding the Nature of Science

If a man will begin with certainties, he shall end in doubts; but if he will be content to begin with doubts, he shall end in certainties.

(Francis Bacon, The Advancement of Learning, 1605)

Science, in its purest translation from the original Latin, *scientia,* means 'knowledge'. The Latin root of the modern-day term was not associated with the discipline of science as we practise and see it today. Strictly speaking, any knowledge could be thought of as scientific in nature. Across the history of human endeavour we may identify many 'scientists', some are accepted freely as founders of the disciplines we promote in schools, for example Galileo, Newton and Darwin. Others are philosophers who worked in areas that contribute to our understanding of science, such as Francis Bacon, Karl Popper or Thomas Kuhn. Over time, more especially since the advent of the scientific revolution in the seventeenth century, the discipline of science has grown up with associated bodies of knowledge and ways of working, sometimes referred to as 'the scientific method', which is in itself a problematic term (see pages 39–43) since different sciences apply different methods to their working and some even reject the notion that a scientific method exists (Feyerabend, 1975).

Conveying what science is, and what science is not, what questions science can and cannot answer is a fundamental aspect of scientific literacy. The main aim of teaching science in schools should be the development of scientific literacy first and foremost, with the acquisition of scientific knowledge second. Until 2006, there was a tendency for science to be taught from a knowledge acquisition perspective, prompted by way that the national curriculum laid out what the pupils must be taught, a series of subject knowledge statements. Since 2006 there have been successive changes to the science curriculum at key stages 4 then 3 which reverse the priority for teaching promoting the idea of How Science Works (HSW) above the acquisition of knowledge about science. To begin with we need to define what makes a subject a 'science' and how we define what is a scientist?

The study of certain subjects would automatically qualify as 'science' for example biology, chemistry or physics. Those who attain a degree-level qualification in such subjects may earn a bachelor's degree in science (BSc) but would they see themselves as 'scientists'? Some may feel that a true scientist not only holds a qualification in a scientific discipline, but has also worked as a scientist in industry or research. Far from just being three subjects, science as a discipline has many branches. Geology, astronomy and psychology for example feature in school-based science, but not as disciplines in their own right at key stage 3. At GCSE and As/A2 level they are available as separate subjects. Some disciplines, for example biology have a number of related subjects such as environmental science or microbiology. If we move to higher education the range of subjects that qualify as a science mushrooms. Many are laboratory based, but some are non-experimental, non-laboratory-based disciplines such as theoretical physics. Before we can usefully decide what science we should teach to children, we must be clear what we mean by a scientist and science, what the subject encompasses and how we may approach the teaching of that subject in a school setting. Most importantly we must understand why we teach science in schools.

In being interviewed for the post of a Head of Science in a secondary school, many candidates may be asked by the interviewing panel to justify why we should teach science and why such a large proportion of the curriculum time available should be devoted to science. After all, science departments are expensive. In capital costs they consume a significant proportion of a school budget per head of pupil. There is the basic science equipment, microscopes, power packs, radioactive sources, expensive/cheap chemicals, expensive/cheap glassware etc. Science requires technical support, special arrangements for health and safety, specialist accommodation and, not least, specialist teachers.

So how justified is the inclusion of science as a major component of the school curriculum? Science as a discipline is much more than merely knowledge of atoms, forces, cells, the earth and the universe. As a discipline it has methodologies that are about investigating and problem solving and a theory base that explains natural phenomena. Ideally what we wish to achieve in teaching science in schools is scientific literacy. In understanding the nature of science we must necessarily look at its history and development and learn something about those who have worked in the past and who currently work in the realms of science, the scientist.

The notion of a scientist

Using the definition above, a scientist is someone who 'knows'. How our pupils perceive scientists may include scientists being 'know-alls', but studies of pupils' perceptions of science and scientists using a DAST (Draw-a-Scientist Test) activity, have typically shown that they are often driven by stereotypical images consisting of white, male, middle-class characters, often grey-haired, balding and with glasses (Quita, 2003; Buldu, 2006). Yet it seems that while these images may contain references to the tools of science, such as the inclusion of scientific instruments to help reinforce the image of a scientist for example a microscope or test tubes, the notion of how scientists work or operate and how they develop understanding of the phenomena they observe is absent. For most children, how scientists work is dominated by where they popularly think scientists work, in a laboratory. This is reinforced by a pupil's own experience of science at secondary school level where the activity of science or science lessons almost always takes place in a laboratory setting, regardless of the content of the lesson, which may not require any specialist teaching facilities. Furthermore, the lack of practical opportunities for pupils and the declining quality of laboratory provision has been identified as contributing to the lack of uptake of science at post 16. In its evidence to the House of Lords

Select Committee on Science and Technology, the Association for Science Education (ASE) stated that *'practical work has become routine and uninspiring so that, rather than engaging students with the excitement of science, such experiences contribute to students considering science as "boring"'* (ASE, 2006). It paints a damming picture of the current state of school science laboratories as unfit for the purpose of teaching science in many cases. Even where some refurbishment and investment in upgrading facilities has taken place, the results do not always meet the demands of teaching science that will fulfil the programme of study requirements (ASE, 2006). The assumption from reading the ASE evidence is that the most effective science is taught in a laboratory setting and through a practical-based curriculum. This view is also endorsed by the National Science Teachers Association (NSTA) of North America *'Laboratory experience is so integral to the nature of science that it must be included in every science program for every student'* (NSTA, 2006). This is not necessarily how science, or indeed how scientists, work on a day-to-day basis. Although the practical, laboratory-based, experimental basis of science cannot be denied, the degree to which all scientists undertake day-to-day practical and experimental work to further their knowledge and understanding is something which cannot easily be measured. The theoretical physicist spends much of his or her time developing mathematical models to explain known phenomena. The astronomer is a largely observational scientist where the chance to set up and 'run' an experiment, in the traditional sense, is limited by the nature of the phenomena under study, phenomena that happen vast distances away from earth and on a huge scale, too big for standard laboratory study. The ASE and NSTA acknowledge that the term 'laboratory' can be limiting. They include reference to working in the environment and working in the community as equally valid 'practical experiences'. There is, however, in both organizations a seeming lack of consideration of the notion of science as a non-practical endeavour, for example the philosophy of science; the process of deduction, induction and inference as logical processes and the benefits instruction in the process of logical argument may have in improving pupils' understanding of how real science works and, more specifically, how scientists work.

Thinking only about where a scientist works is limiting. Even knowing that many scientists for example geologists, environmental scientists, work 'in the field' collecting specimens and data, these scientists also have lab work as an integral part of their day-to-day working conditions. All scientists will, how-ever, spend time conducting research through reading books and journals and modelling their ideas physically, mathematically or virtually. Computers and computer work now play a significant role in scientific endeavour. Should our notion of what a scientist is change due to the way in which many scientists now work? We cannot neglect that the fields of science expand as disciplines within previously broad areas of science develop their own body of knowl-edge. Whereas biology superficially may look at any and all aspects of living organisms, the discipline now incorporates a wide range of fields from micro-biology to ichthyology, entomology etc. The scientists working in these disci-plines will have developed their own protocols and methodologies which, while related to a general idea of how scientists work, will differ in detail. The problem for school science is how do we capture the essence of what a scientist is without being too prescriptive or too loose in our definition? More impor-tantly, how do we provide a coherent vision for How Science Works in the face of the current 'old' and 'new' programmes of study?

The notion of the scientific method, though implied in the curriculum, for example in 'practical and enquiry skills' the first key process of the new pro-gramme of study at key stage 3, is neither fully explored nor expanded upon explicitly as a theoretical underpinning to How Science Works, yet 'scientific method' is specifically mentioned in the QCA definition of HSW (QCA, 2006). The key processes now include the requirement for pupils to have a critical understanding of evidence and to know how to communicate science. The key concepts which underpin science at key stage 3 include scientific thinking, the applications and implications of science and a cultural understanding of science and its roots. Contrast this, however with the key stage 2 programme of study which remains unchanged from earlier versions of the national cur-riculum and has, as its first attainment target, ideas and evidence in science and investigative skills at its heart. Key stage 4, which should naturally flow on from key stage 3, contains the first mention of How Science Works, first looking at data, evidence, theories and explanations followed by practical and enquiry skills, moving to communication skills culminating in the applica-tions and implications of science. While there have been major revisions and move to process-based teaching from fact-based teaching in science, there appears to be a lack of 'joined up thinking' in how the new key stage 3 inte-grates with the previously introduced key stage 4 and the 'old' key stages 1 and 2.

Science though is still a core subject which must be delivered to all pupils to the end of key stage 4. As such science has a degree of authority. Is this reflected though in the public perception of science and scientists?

The authority of science

The kudos of science, sometimes of individual scientists, or the authority that science can bring to any study or any publication, is very attractive. So much so that science, sometimes, sadly, pseudoscience, is included in advertising on television and radio and in newspaper reports. At times the science used by journalists and reporters is incorrect, not actually science at all, or it is simply bad science. In a popular newspaper column, Dr Ben Goldacre, a medical scientist, exposes poor science and pseudoscience. Often the description of an expert as a 'scientist' instils a sense of authority and an aura of trust and truthfulness which the public at large relies upon for definitive statements about key aspects of controversial issues, for example global warming, cloning or the safety of medicines. With the era of mass communication now upon us, science is being exposed to more hard-hitting questions. Rival groups employ their own experts to contradict evidence presented to the public with which they disagree, from time to time the disagreement is philosophical not just about contradictory evidence or different interpretations of evidence.

How scientists work and what constitutes science is increasingly important. One aspect of why we should teach science as a core subject is about just this issue. Educating young people about what science is, how scientists operate and how science works is fundamental to creating and maintaining a scientifically literate society. In the next section we will look at what we mean by science and define the discipline of science as it applies to schools.

The discipline of science

The exact origin of science as a discipline is an intangible thing. There is no one defining moment that we can point to where 'science' began. Humans are curious animals. That curiosity would have been haphazard in the earliest days of human existence. No attempt at structuring the knowledge gained from crude experiments – not that those conducting investigations into their natural surroundings would have the notion that what they were doing was an experiment – would have taken place. Learning would, most likely, be experiential with the knowledge passed down orally, sometimes pictorially. As individuals and groups gained knowledge about the natural world, it would have been passed down to future generations remaining as localized knowledge. As cultures and civilizations grew the localized knowledge would become more widespread. As civilizations gained the means to travel larger distances knowledge and understanding of the natural world would also travel. Until ancient civilizations developed more sophisticated cultures where the systematic recording of knowledge could take place science as a discipline could not really exist.

As we know, science means knowledge. As a definition this lacks depth and sophistication. This definition would not help pupils of any age get to grips with what science is and what science is not. Chambers Dictionary of Science and Technology defines science as '*The ordered arrangement of ascertained knowledge, including the methods by which such knowledge is extended and the criteria by which its truth is tested*' (Walker, 1999). Two parts of this definition are interesting for our purposes. The definition includes the term 'methods' rather than method, indicating that perhaps our notion of THE scientific method, or the idea of just one way of doing science is incorrect. The majority of practicing scientists would concur with this view. How science is done varies. The other interesting aspect of this definition is the notion of 'truth' in science. Colloquially we often talk about scientific proof and the notion of something being true because it is accepted scientific knowledge. The notion of proof and truth in science will be discussed briefly in the next section. The Chambers definition is not entirely helpful to us when considering definitions of science that are appropriate for school-based teaching and learning. The Concise Oxford Dictionary (Thompson, 1995) defines science as '*The branch of knowledge conducted on objective principles involving the systematized observation of, and experiment with, phenomena, esp. concerned with the material and functions of the physical universe*' (p. 1237). This is more akin to what we think of as a definition of science. It includes the idea of experiment and restricts the study of science to the physical universe. Other definitions of the term science in the Concise Oxford Dictionary also apply the idea of a systematic body of knowledge in other fields, such as politics, hence producing the notion of political science.

If our definition of 'science' meant that whatever we study must be tangible and directly observable then many aspects of sub-atomic physics, for example the existence of sub-atomic particles such as bosons, quarks etc. would be ruled out of science. Our definition of science must allow for what is currently unobservable, but accepted in principle. If we define science as including 'experimentation', again, aspects of what is accepted science, but which cannot be demonstrated by traditional notions of experiments in laboratory or natural settings, would also be ruled out. Our definition of science then must encompass the wide range of currently accepted scientific disciplines.

In 1999 the American Association for the Advancement of Science published *Science for All Americans* (Rutherford and Ahlgren, 1991). Its aim was to increase scientific literacy. There was recognition that a good science education is vital to the well being of any country.

> *Science, energetically pursued, can provide humanity with the knowledge of the biophysical environment and of social behavior (sic) needed to develop effective solutions to its global and local problems; without that knowledge, progress toward a safe world will be unnecessarily handicapped.*
>
> (Rutherford and Ahlgren, 1991)

Once we have an agreed definition of what science means, we must turn our attention to how science operates and what science can and cannot do. The next section looks at the notions of truth and proof in science and what these terms mean.

The notion of proof and truth in science

The headlines in newspapers are designed to entice readers into the story. Scientists find a cure for cancer; drinking too much alcohol is bad for you; not drinking alcohol is bad for you. There are often confusing messages delivered in the media. The stories often contain phrases such as 'science proves'. Before we fully tackle how science works or how scientists work we need to understand what we mean by 'truth' and 'proof' in science.

Just as many scientific words have common meanings which could confuse children, certain words have subtly different meanings in science. 'Proof' and 'truth' have specific connotations and meanings in science.

> 'Proof' in science does not mean 'certainty' or 'absolute truth' but only 'proof relative to a given body of evidence.' This does not imply, of course, that scientific

theories and hypotheses have no support at all, since we have very good reasons
for believing that the earth is not flat, that dinosaurs existed, and that DNA carries
genetic information.

(Resnick, 1996)

Science is viewed by many as definitive, basing its conclusions on facts
and that it can deliver answers to questions and problem. Scientists do not
start from the premise of science being about universal 'truths' or definitive
answers. Any person working in the realm of science understands that the idea
of truth in science is also relative. The mistake happens when people consider
the pursuit of science to be the pursuit of truth. Science can often result in
a confused understanding of the world. If we take light for example, is it a
wave or a particle? What is the 'true' nature of light? Is it a mixture of waves
and particles or is the way in which we try to make sense of light, by categoriz-
ing its essential features according to properties that fit a wave model or a
particle model, that is getting in the way of our understanding of its real or
'true' form?

Surely though, some things in science can be thought of as true. Science is,
after all, filled with facts and these should be 'true'. The problem for science
is that facts are not necessarily unchanging. Were we to chart the development
of certain scientific theories over time we would see how new evidence
obtained from the gathering of data (facts) changes our interpretations. For
example, the apparent 'fit' of the continents (e.g. the fit that could be obtained
by juxtaposing South America and Africa) has been explained in the past
using a number of ideas. The data showed that at one time South America and
Africa were indeed joined in geological history – the similarity in fossil fauna
and flora, the chemical and stratigraphical similarity between the rocks inevitably led to the conclusion that the two land masses were at one time linked.
It was also a 'fact' that the continents did not move, so ideas had to be developed to explain the 'fit'. One idea was that it was a sheer coincidence – but the
fossils and rocks were at odds with this idea. Another was that there existed at
one time land bridges between the two continents which could explain the
fossil flora and fauna and the continuity of rock types. This leaves the question,
what happened to this 'bridge' – how and why is it no longer in place and what
evidence do we have that it ever existed? The land bridge idea was also used to
explain the lost continent/city/country of Atlantis. A third idea was that the
earth was expanding and that the shapes, rocks and fossils provided evidence
for the expanding earth. Some facts would fit all the ideas, but plate tectonics

provided a better explanation than any of the others. When geophysical data gathered from the sea floor provided evidence that this 'continental drift' was not due to an expanding earth, but due to the movement of crustal plates over the surface of the earth with new rock forming along mid-oceanic ridges, the theory of plate tectonics was born and the expanding earth theory effectively killed off. An expanding earth may have explained how land, once covered by the sea, is now remote from the shore, but it did not explain how seas can invade lands, a phenomenon clearly shown in our geological history. If our earth is expanding, why don't electricity cables, telephone lines and transatlantic undersea cables break more often as they become stretched between continents that are moving apart? If the earth is expanding why do we have subduction zones which mean that continents move towards one another in some areas and constructive margins where new rock forces the Earth's surface apart in others, such as the mid-Atlantic ridge? Finally how could we account for the necessary increase in the mass of the Earth needed to fill the internal 'void' created by expansion? If the void is filled by a collapse of the oceanic crust then surely the ocean basins would accommodate more water and the seas would retreat further from the coasts.

Science holds its theories to be 'true and proven' under specific circumstances. Science can never state anything with absolute certainty. This causes a problem for us all. We need to hold certain ideas as true and proven in order to carry out our work. Often we come to an arrangement where, for operational reasons, we accept certain things without continually questioning their status, for example we accept that the force of gravity means that objects fall to earth at a rate of 9.81ms^{-2}. We understand that this is an average measurement. For school science it is often rounded to 10ms^{-2}. The reality of acceleration due to gravity is that this figure will vary according to local conditions, for example it is less off the South coast of India than in the Pacific region. Your mass is approximately 1 per cent less off the coast of India when compared to the average. Also, objects will be affected by air resistance and will not immediately fall at a constant speed when they are released. Science has developed a body of knowledge and a way of working that can cope with this uncertainty and science is always ready to accept the abandonment of ideas when contrary evidence is overwhelming. Individual scientists may cling to outdated ideas and others may struggle to introduce new ideas, but on the whole science works because it is not a fixed body of incontrovertible facts.

References

ASE, 2006. *Science Teaching in Schools.* In: TECHNOLOGY, H. O. L. S. C. O. S. A. (ed.). London: ASE.

Buldu, M. 2006. *Young Children's Perceptions of Scientists: A Preliminary Study. Educational Research,* 48, 121–132.

Feyerabend, P. K. 1975. *Against Method,* London: Verso.

NSTA, 2006. *NSTA Position Statement* [Online]. NSTA. Available: http://www.nsta.org/position-statement&psid=16 [Accessed].

Quita, I. 2003. *What Is a Scientist? Perspectives of Teachers of Color. Multicultural Education,* 11, 29–31.

Rutherford, J. and Ahlgren, A. 1991. *Science for All Americans,* Oxford: Oxford University Press.

Thompson, D. (ed.) 1995. *The Concise Oxford Dictionary,* Oxford: Oxford University Press.

Walker, P. (ed.) 1999. *Chambers Dictionary of Science and Technology,* Edinburgh: Chambers Harrap.

Further reading

Chalmers, A. 1999. *What Is This Thing Called Science?* Milton Keynes: Open University Press.

Goldacre, B. 2008. *Bad Science.* London: Forth Estate.

Kuhn, T. 1996. *The Structure of Scientific Revolutions.* Chicago: University of Chicago Press.

A Brief History of Science   2

Chapter Outline

Science taught . . . without a sense of history is robbed of those very qualities that make it worth teaching to the student of the humanities and social sciences.

(Bernard Cohen (1914–2003) historian of science)

It could be argued that the question 'why' defines humans from other living organisms. Humans are inquisitive, that is not to say that animals are not, but the difference is that humans ask 'why' whereas animals, to the best of our knowledge, do not. Animals may learn from experience, but humans investigate the underlying causes of natural phenomena. Why does each year appear to have seasons? Why does the earth appear to be motionless and the sun revolve around it? Why do different types of animals and plants live in different habitats? In some ways what humans are doing is linking cause and effect, *'if this happens, then this results'*. Crucial to that linking is the idea of prediction. Humans try to predict from their observations of events and processes. Alongside such passive activities as observation and prediction, humans also are novel for their investigations of the properties of the natural world. Chance happenings, serendipitous events, systematic exploration and experimentation have all played their part in the history of humankind and, as such, in the history of science. The disciplines of science that are in operation today are not naturally created disciplines but ones which humankind has created. The natural world does not differentiate between biology and biochemistry, physics and quantum physics. Humankind has, over thousands of years, developed and compartmentalized knowledge to form the discipline we call science. Some aspects and areas in science are relatively recent innovations, for example, the science of 'biology' was only named as such in the early nineteenth century, by Jean Baptiste Lamarck (of alternative evolutionary theory fame), but that is not the start of the study of living things. Aristotle, for example, first began describing and classifying living organisms in Greek times. The exact origin of the sciences is often lost in time. Today, 'new' sciences are established with their origins being relatively well documented, for example, nanoscience.

We must also make a distinction between science – knowledge of the natural world – and technology, the application of science to solving problems. Nanoscience, a recent discipline, is concerned with study at an atomic or molecular level and nanotechnology is the application of nanoscience to solving real-world problems. Each discipline has a history and this chapter will look at some of the major events in the history of science.

Magic or science?

For ancient humans, the distinction between magic and science would have been non-existent. Evoking prayers or performing rituals to encourage rain for crops to grow or appeasing the Gods with the slaughter of animals, even humans, to prevent natural disasters to modern civilization looks silly, even barbaric. Making connections between volcanic eruptions and upsetting some mythical supernatural being has no place in science today. Yet although we understand the broad mechanisms whereby plate movements can cause volcanic eruptions, we still cannot with any degree of predictive power or accuracy, know when an eruption is likely to take place. Devastating events, for example in Haiti and Chile where large earthquakes caused immense damage and the deaths of many thousands of people, can still have modern communities offering prayers for the survivors and, for those who tragically lost their lives. So just what is the difference between offering prayers to a God to prevent a volcanic eruption and offering prayers for the survivors of a natural disaster? We may laugh at the shaman performing a rain dance and glibly say that meteorology is a far better way of predicting when the rains may come for the crops, yet meteorology's record in accurate long-range forecasting is not good.

In early 2010 the Met Office in the United Kingdom decided to drop long-range forecasting of the British weather in favour of monthly forecasts, updated weekly (Derbyshire, 2010). This came after embarrassing forecasts of a 'barbeque' summer in 2009 and a mild winter across late 2009 early 2010. Both predictions were not just a little wrong, the winter was the coldest in nearly 30 years. Despite many years of scientific study, science can only beat shamanic approaches with short-term forecasting. It seems that being able to make long-range weather forecasts is still a case where magic can be as successful as science.

What made the magician of ancient times successful is most likely their ability to observe nature and to form reasonably accurate short-term predictions. Their predictions need not have been 100 per cent accurate. Look today at generalized predictions in astrology and consider how many people subscribe to their future being foretold 'in the stars' and it is easy to see that a shaman or ancient mystic need only be marginally better at making predictions than the general population to be seen as 'magical'. They would appear to have powers and connections with the supernatural. In reality they were simply being scientists, observing the natural world, forming hypotheses, making predictions and, should their predictions be correct or nearly so, they would refine and confirm their original finding and move towards an explanation – a 'theory'– for that natural phenomenon. The mystic, the shaman of ancient times was no less a scientist than the meteorologist or volcanologist today. Time changes our perspective on science and scientists, but to understand where we are today we need a sense of where we have come from.

Stone-age technology or science?

Pre-history can be broadly separated into three phases. The first of these ages was the Stone Age – where stone tools were used for a variety of purposes from hunting to building with primitive (though sophisticated for their day) axes, hammers and flints. The construction of these artefacts is clearly evidence of technological advances, though whether they show 'scientific' awareness is less clear. The stone-age tool makers would doubtless have had knowledge of rock types and their characteristics. You could even argue that they would have experimented with shapes and techniques to produce their various implements. There is evidence of a trade in technology and artefacts, but this may not constitute an 'origin' of scientific thinking and endeavour as the systematic recording of that knowledge and understanding and of the technology used is nowhere evident.

The Stone Age is a term that varies in its definition and covers a wide range of pre-historic time. The precise start of the Stone Age is subject to revision as new evidence comes to light. Early hominids (e.g. *Homo habilis*) used stone tools some 2.5–2.6 million years ago (MYA) during the early Palaeolithic. The Stone Age ends in the Neolithic some 12,000 years ago.

Origins of scientific discovery

Ten thousand years or so ago there is evidence that populations in the Middle East used their knowledge and understanding of plants for food and medicine. This is not unique. The use of herbal remedies apparently goes back 60,000 years as can be seen from evidence uncovered in 1960 of a Neanderthal skeleton buried with various species of plants, some of which are still used today as medicinal. The burial was uncovered in a cave in present-day Iraq, the Shanidar cave (Solecki et al., 2004). Whether this burial represents a ritual with and knowledge of the use of plants in a medicinal capacity has been debated (Sommer, 1999). If it does, then this is an example of scientific knowledge and thinking. The Shanidar cave is also the inspiration for the novel *The Clan of the Cave Bear*; extracts from the book could, of course, be used to discuss how scientific are the descriptions of life in the Shanidar cave and how much scientific evidence could contribute to a fictional novel (a technique that can be used with a number of science-based/related novels for example *Jurassic Park*).

Controversially, if we accept that Neanderthals do not have a direct lineage with modern-day humans you could argue that scientific discovery is not a unique human trait.

What was unique some 10,000 years ago was the description of plants, not merely those used for food or medicine, but just for their intrinsic value. Also, animals were categorized and described. Gathering such knowledge is different from utilizing the properties of plants and animals for food or medicine. Here then, arguably, is one origin of scientific discovery – that is related to the modern-day discipline of biology.

Metals and the origin of chemistry

The early metallurgists of the bronze and iron ages can be thought of as the early chemists. Their knowledge and understanding of the chemistry and extraction of these metals from the rocks in which they were found was by no means a systematic and considered process which followed the conventions of how chemists today would operate. Exactly how these civilizations discovered and modified the process of extraction is unknown. The most likely 'method' was trial and error: what, for those times we could consider experimentation.

Exactly where and how bronze came into being is also a mystery. How ancient metallurgists hit upon the formula of 10 parts copper to 1 part tin to create a composite alloy that was so useful and influential is not easily answered. Deposits of copper and tin today are not found in large amounts side by side. It is possible that in the early Bronze Age naturally occurring tin deposits (cassiterite) were initially used and they were exhausted relatively quickly, leading to exploration and trading for new untapped deposits. The Bronze Age (3,300 BCE–1,200 BCE) is a key time in human development as it allowed humans for the first time to produce durable tools that better served their purposes than the more crude stone implements. The Anatolia (Turkish) region lying south of the Black Sea, east of the Aegean Sea, and north of the eastern Mediterranean Sea is often cited as the birthplace of bronze-age tool making and technology.

Pre-history medicine

Early humankind observed that certain plants could be used to treat sickness and disease. They developed herbal medicines and, with the domestication of animals and the routine growing of crops, came knowledge and understanding of disease. With it, came cures for some of those diseases. Domestication of animals started around 7,000 BCE and it is reasonable to assume that the early farmers saw and treated many diseases and injuries. Such treatment may have come from the early treatment of other humans. Helping domesticated animals in the birth process would have used knowledge and understanding of helping fellow humans who gave birth. The early farmer would have been able to see similarities and differences between human and animal birth processes and used a knowledge and understanding of helping others give birth to help animals produce healthy livestock which would be beneficial to the community as a whole.

A very early surgical procedure – and a very surprising one – was trepanning (also known as trephining). It involved the drilling of a hole in the skull to treat a variety of ailments and illnesses. Evidence of trepanning has been found in pre-history human remains, going back to 2,000 BCE, with a female skull discovered in Armenia that had a one-inch hole plugged with animal bone. Evidence of active growth around the bone plug and the hole shows that the patient survived the 'surgery' (Prioreschi, 1991). Trepanning and herbal medicine were probably not the result of scientific endeavour as we would appreciate it today. Drilling holes in the skull to 'release demons' (one reason that trepanning is thought to have been practised), when the 'demons' were probably epileptic fits, was unlikely to have been the result of a scientific investigation of epilepsy and how to prevent it. Even in the Bible there is evidence of epilepsy. In a story recounted in the Gospel of Mark, Jesus is said to have 'cast out a devil' from a young man. The description of the possession of this man fits well with the symptoms of epilepsy; falling to the ground, foaming at the mouth and the body becoming rigid. Modern explanations of epilepsy are a result of scientific investigations which determined that seizures are caused by bursts of excess electrical activity in the brain. These can cause temporary disruptions to the normal messages that pass across the synapses between brain cells. Modern science does not advocate trepanning as a cure, with most forms of epilepsy being treated with some form of medication. Interestingly epilepsy is now being treated with surgery, which involves a range of invasive brain techniques, with increasingly positive results. While modern brain surgery is nothing like pre-historic trepanning, the ultimate goal – the removal of brain tissue which may be the cause of fitting – remains the same.

In some ways trepanning, where a small hole is drilled, is 'minor' when compared with modern-day brain surgery where the skull cap is effectively removed then replaced and stapled back into place.

Greek and Egyptian science

A goal of science is to provide explanations of natural phenomena. The first people to try and develop such systematic explanations were the Greeks: Aristotle, for example, classified plants and animals – he set up one of the first classification systems and this system remained in use for many centuries. Others, for example Pythagoras, concentrated on a mathematical view of the world providing us with his theorem concerning right-angled triangles ($a^2 + b^2 = c^2$). Aristotle and Plato, Aristotle's teacher, developed methods for examining the world around them laying the foundation of logical thinking. Around 460 BCE, Democritus developed the idea of atoms. His thought process, leading to the idea that matter was made up of fundamental particles called atoms, took the form of a question: how often can you break a piece of matter in half before you can no longer break it in half again? Logically he thought, there must come a point where the matter is so small it cannot be broken down any further. The particles that you have at this point he called atoms. Interestingly, Aristotle, a very influential Greek figure, did not lend his support to Democritus' idea. In effect his ideas were dismissed. It took another 2,000 years, until the nineteenth century, before scientists were ready and able to investigate the structure of matter at the atomic level.

Thales of Miletus

One of the founders of Greek science is the philosopher Thales of Miletus (approx. 624–547 BCE). Thales thought that the earth floated on water. For him, everything came from water. He thought of the earth as a flat disc floating on an infinite sea. Thales used this to explain how earthquakes happened. Ripples in the water would cause the earth to shake and this explained earthquakes. Thales was wrong, but this was not the point. Thales was the first person to try and explain phenomena using natural causations rather than supernatural causations, that is the anger of the Gods shaking the earth as the cause of earthquakes.

It is easy to focus on the Greeks and their foundations for our current scientific thinking, but the progress of science was also aided by developments in China, South America, India and the Middle East. The invention of gunpowder, widely attributed to the Chinese in the ninth century (Gray et al., 1982), made its way to other civilizations. This discovery was very influential in world politics and supremacy. Other discoveries, though lesser in their destructive impact and power, such as soap and paper were, nonetheless influential.

In ancient Egypt, science and medicine was advanced, yet also naive. Many ancient papyri survive that detail many medical procedures, treatment cures and diagnoses. Other papyri (magical) show the less advanced side of Egyptian life. There is no doubt that the Egyptians had sophisticated techniques for embalming and dealing with their dead. Even common everyday ailments were documented.

> In magical papyri, headaches are attributed to the action of demons and supernatural forces, whereas medical papyri emphasize the role of head trauma and of 'pain matter' occurring in the body. Treatment could be magical, pharmacological or surgical.
>
> (Karenberg and Leitz, 2001)

In ancient Egypt magic and science coexisted.

Bringing together the knowledge and understanding that characterized early scientific discoveries did not happen until the foundation of the universities. Often scientific knowledge such as the 'recipe' for gunpowder or soap was passed by word of mouth, or inscribed into or onto tablets of clay or stone for example in the case of a recipe for soap manufacture, into a Mesopotamian clay tablet dating back to 2,200 BCE.

From the establishment of the early university system in Europe, around the thirteenth century and for the next 300 years science and scientific thinking made slow, but important progress.

The birth of modern science: the scientific revolution

Sir Francis Bacon (1561–1626) is one of the prime figures of the so-called scientific revolution (Ronan, 1983; Williams, 2007; Gribbin, 2002). Alongside Newton and Galileo he holds a position in the history of science that has been seen as influential for many generations of scientists (Gribbin, 2002: 134). This is not because of his work as an experimental scientist, since this was one aspect of his work that was lacking, but in the arena of the development of a philosophical approach to science. Bacon performed few actual 'experiments'; his influential position stems from promoting the study of science by gathering data and then, by inference or inductive reasoning, coming to conclusions.

In addition to examining the world and using logic to deduce, infer or explain phenomena, instrumentation played a vital part in scientific discovery allowing philosopher–scientists to more closely examine the world, life and the universe. Telescopes provided more and more information about the solar system and the position of our planet; microscopes gave close-up views of insects, plants and animals; clocks could measure time and barometers provided measurements of the atmosphere. Science became more organized and the ability to record the observations made by the eye and the new instrumentation allowed generalizations about phenomena to be made. Those generalizations resulted in scientific laws. Newton's universal Law of gravitation, describing how gravity acts is a good case in point. Scientific laws of the seventeenth century described phenomena, they did not explain them. The laws were generalizations that knew no exceptions, hence their designation as scientific laws. Many of those laws are still in use today though for some laws, the idea of 'without exception' does not currently hold. In Chapter 4 the idea of Laws, theories, hypotheses, principles and facts will be looked into in more detail and some of the web of confusion that arises over the use of this terminology untangled.

Scientific progress and the age of enlightenment

The scientific revolution of the seventeenth century led into the industrial revolution of the eighteenth century. This period, also known as the 'age of enlightenment', sees the first widespread use of reason to provide explanations for natural phenomena, hence enlightenment. It was not just the application of reason to solve what are inherently 'scientific' problems that characterizes the age of enlightenment. Many social problems also had 'reason' applied to them. People such as John Locke (1632–1704), a philosopher who also studied medicine, but didn't qualify, was influenced by scientists of the day such as Robert Boyle (1627–1691), assisting him in his experiments. Voltaire (1694–1778), poet, novelist, philosopher and scientist, is the man who introduced the world to the story of Newton and the apple in his *Elements de la Philosophie de Newton*, published in 1738, 73 years after Newton's death. It is clear from his writing that Voltaire had a great respect for Newton and his work. The demarcation between science, philosophy and the arts was not as clear-cut as it is today.

From the invention of the mercury thermometer by Gabriel Fahrenheit to the discovery of lightening as electrical phenomena by Benjamin Franklin; Lavoisier's and Priestley's discovery of oxygen, replacing phlogiston theory; Georges Cuvier's establishment of extinction of species in the geological past and William Herschel's discovery of Uranus, all characterize a period of fast growth in scientific knowledge and understanding. It also provides a firm base for yet more scientific discovery and understanding in the nineteenth century.

The evolution of science and the science of evolution

The nineteenth century provides us with a plethora of scientists, many of whose names are familiar to the general public: Darwin and Wallace, Lamarck, Dalton, Faraday, Maxwell, Thompson, Ohm and Joule. Some of these names are now rightly synonymous with units named in their honour (such as Ohm and Joule). Others supply us not just with scientific laws, such as Amedeo Avogadro (1776–1856), but also with a constant – Avogadro's number – 6.023 $\times 10.^{23}$ Children, and the general public often use these names without reference to or knowledge of the person behind the discovery. Conversely some scientists, whose names are inextricably linked to theories, concepts or ideas such as Darwin (and the less widely known Alfred Russel Wallace) maintain a high profile in the public's (and in our pupils') minds. A misunderstanding or misinterpretation of Darwin and Wallace's theory of evolution by means of natural selection is touted as controversial. Yet an examination of the facts and evidence surrounding biological evolution shows it to be no more controversial than the acceptance of gravity or atoms. Few ideas court as much controversy as evolution, yet the basis for many nineteenth-century ideas was accepted with less scientific evidence.

Major revolutions in scientific thinking and discovery are not restricted to history. Major scientific discoveries, from the discovery of the structure of DNA by Crick and Watson in 1953, to the description of plate tectonics in a unified form in the 1960s, continue to be made and will continue as science seeks to understand and explain natural phenomena.

Conclusion

This chapter started with a quotation that urges us to teach about the history and philosophy of science, to expose the 'grandeur' of discovery. I would argue that the history of science is the very hook upon which good science today could hang. Understanding how ideas have developed over time, how evidence which contradicts a prevailing idea (e.g. natural selection over the inheritance of acquired characteristics) allows our pupils to see not just the limitations of science, but also the strength of science as an evidence-based discipline where guessing or playing a hunch does not play a part in explaining natural phenomena, though it may be the initial starting point to discovering explanations. The temptation when using the history of science is to look back at the nineteenth, eighteenth or any past age through the lens of the twenty-first century. Ideas such as spontaneous generation of life – or life (mice) appearing from sweaty socks – can be a source of amusement and ridicule in science lessons. The key is to try and look at the discoveries and ideas from the perspective of the scientist/philosopher of that time. Think about the social and cultural restraints. Consider the lack of instrumentation or the limitations of the technology of the day to solve problems. Only then will the true genius of people such as Newton be understood. The historical perspective also provides for an examination of the human face of science. Science is, at its heart, a human endeavour. It is not something that occurs naturally. With human endeavour come human failings. Newton by all accounts, was not the nicest of people. He was very religious, but he was also an alchemist – searching for the philosopher's stone. He made mistakes in his work, yet he also provided us with the basis of modern physics through his universal laws of gravitation. He lends his name to the measurement of weight and his particular approach to physics is called Newtonian physics as opposed to the more modern synthesis we call Einsteinian physics. They coexist yet are fundamentally different: Newtonian physics, the science of the big – how gravity operates on the planets – to Einsteinian physics – the science of the very small – what's happening inside the atom. The prize for all physicists would be the unification of these two scientific paradigms. The prize for biology would be the discovery of the origin of life; for astronomy, the origin of the universe. Understanding the history of science provides a setting for contemporary science. Knowing where we have come from provides us with the sense of the journey that ultimately we would like some of our pupils to carry on.

Reflective task

The history of science charts the development of ideas over time. Each of the scientific disciplines will have central ideas that have been developed over time. Review the content areas for science at KS3 and 4 and identify these central ideas, then produce a timeline (verbal or illustrated) which could be used as a resource in the classroom to illustrate how science changes and develops over time. Include in the teaching schemes lessons which incorporate these ideas to illustrate to pupils the historical aspect of science and how science works.

Classroom task

Science today can explain much more about the natural world than scientists hundreds of years ago. Choose a scientist from the history of science and write them a letter explaining how their idea has been developed over time and how their idea is now part of the school curriculum. You will need to point out to the scientist what we now know that they didn't know when they made their discovery and what the evidence is that we have which either confirms what they thought or which contradicts what they thought.

References

Derbyshire, D. 2010. Met Office drops long-term forecasts after fiasco of last year's predictions | Mail Online. *Daily Mail*, 6 March 2010.

Gray, E., Marsh, H. and McLaren, M. 1982. A short history of gunpowder and the role of charcoal in its manufacture. *Journal of Materials Science,* 17, 3385–3400.

Gribbin, J. 2002. *Science: A History 1543–2001,* London: Allen Lane.

Karenberg, A. and Leitz, C. 2001. Headache in magical and medical papyri of Ancient Egypt. *Cephalalgia,* 21, 911–916.

Prioreschi, P. 1991. Possible reasons for Neolithic skull trephining. *Perspectives in Biology and Medicine,* 34, 296–303.

Ronan, C. A. 1983. *The Cambridge Illustrated History of the World's Science,* Cambridge: Cambridge University Press.

Solecki, R. S., Solecki, R. L. and Agelarakis, A. P. 2004. *The Proto-Neolithic Cemetery in Shanidar Cave (Texas A&M University Anthology Series),* Texas: Texas A & M University Press.

Sommer, J. D. 1999. The Shanidar IV? Flower burial?: A re-evaluation of Neanderthal burial ritual. *Cambridge Archaeological Journal,* 9, 127–129.

Williams, J. D. 2007. Do we know how science works? A brief history of the scientific method. *School Science Review,* 89, 119–124.

Further reading

Bryson, B. 2003. *A Short History of Nearly Everything,* London: Doubleday.

Gribbin, J. 2002. *Science: A History 1543–2001,* London: Allen Lane.

3 What Makes Science 'Science'?

Chapter Outline

Scientia potestas est (knowledge is power).

(Francis Bacon (1561–1626) essayist and philosopher)

In Chapter 1, a definition of science was given from the Concise Oxford Dictionary: *The branch of knowledge conducted on objective principles involving the systematized observation of, and experiment with, phenomena, esp. concerned with the material and functions of the physical universe* (Thompson, 1995: 1237). Defining science does not necessarily provide us with an understanding of what science is. The definition helpfully provides some parameters for science, but it does not tell us what makes the knowledge scientific and how we may usefully distinguish science from pseudoscience. This chapter outlines the thoughts of historians and philosophers of science on what makes science 'science'. You could be forgiven for thinking that this will have little relevance to the idea of How Science Works in the classroom, but aspects of the philosophy of science are present in the approaches we take to science in real life – understanding how scientists work as opposed to how science works.

The definition of science, from the original Latin, is clearly too broad. The idea of science simply as 'knowledge' encompasses every aspect of human endeavour. Even if we narrow this down to 'knowledge of the natural world', this definition is still too broad. Anyone who knows anything at all about the natural world would, by definition, be a scientist. A photographer or painter will 'know' about the natural world, yet we wouldn't classify them as scientists. If we include aspects of the process of science (investigation and experimentation), then we are beginning to look at science as something more than simply knowledge. The process of science – what we could refer to as 'scientific method' – should help us to understand what makes science 'science'. Here, however we hit a major problem. Whose scientific method? Is there just one 'method' or are there several methodologies which combine to make science 'science'? The opening quotation of this book, by Peter Medawar, provides us with the nub of the problem. Often, scientists do not know what makes a science 'science'. There will be disagreement over what the scientific method is (even if one exists at all) and there will be varying views on how science should be defined and taught in schools, even universities. It is worth exploring the view of science across the school system as a starting point for promoting a consolidated view of what science is.

Science in the primary setting

In a primary school setting children now have a good grasp of the notion of a fair test, something that they tend to carry through to secondary science. This aspect of scientific investigation has been present since the inception of science as a formal, compulsory element of primary education. Even before this, primary teachers who understood aspects of scientific investigation could use the notion of a fair test to differentiate for pupils a scientific approach from a non-scientific one.

If we consider the idea of a simple investigation done by primary children at key stage 2, insulation, the majority of children will know that in order for such an investigation to be successful and meaningful, they must keep certain factors (variables) the same, for example the volume of water in a beaker/cup. They may then change other factors such as the type of material being used as an insulator. Initially they will be asked to 'guess' (hypothesize) about which material will be the best insulator. They may also be asked 'why' they think this. Having hypothesized, predicted and determined the variables they will control, the next stage will be to test their ideas. Many primary pupils may indeed identify the 'science' work that they do in terms of the ability to 'test' ideas and from the results of their tests, come to conclusions (explanations) about phenomena.

Secondary science

Here we see a major change to the way science is taught from the approach taken in the primary classroom. The location of the teaching changes, from a classroom to a laboratory. The type of teacher changes, from a generalist to a specialist. How children see science and scientists (as briefly discussed in Chapter 1) is more a product of stereotypes and media image than reality. In secondary science we move from an investigative approach, which may, in turn, be part of a topic approach to teaching in the primary curriculum, to a more formal experimental and investigative approach. Problem solving is common to primary and secondary science teaching, but how those problems are approached and what methods pupils may use to problem solve may well be very different. In short, many primary children do not make explicit connections and links between their study of science in primary settings and at secondary. Many projects that attempt to bridge that divide have also not been that successful (Braund and Hames, 2005), quite interestingly not due to issues to do with the pupils' perceptions of such projects, but more often to do with how teachers view such work.

In moving from the primary to secondary classroom (Braund and Hames, 2005: 782–783) identified 4 key elements from previous studies that hindered progression:

1. Pupils may repeat work done at primary school, often without sufficient increase in challenge, sometimes in the same context and using identical procedures.
2. Teaching environments, teaching styles and teachers' language are often very different in secondary schools compared with primary schools.

3. Teachers in secondary schools often fail to make use of, or refer to, pupils' previous science learning experiences.
4. Teachers in secondary schools distrust the assessed levels of performance gained by pupils in national tests in science.

The recent changes to the science curriculum at secondary level, make now an opportune time to look at how we approach the teaching of science. It would be useful to look carefully at how we shift from a content laden curriculum to one that teaches the content via the process of science. This shift may well help improve the transfer between primary and secondary for pupils and provide teachers with an opportunity to improve the overall scientific literacy of students.

For many, the study of science is a utilitarian pursuit. We study science to be a scientist. The reason for applying to university to study chemistry is, for many, so that the student can become a chemist. Studying science simply because the student finds it an intrinsically interesting subject is probably less of a motivation. This is not the case for many other university subjects. Not all English graduates go on to become novelists and those who study history do not necessarily become historians. In arts subjects often the motivation for study is more linked to intrinsic interest than career progression. It may well be that the fact-based approach to teaching science does not generate the interest in pupils to encourage them to take up sciences at university. Perhaps the process-based approach, looking at science from a philosophical perspective could just encourage interest in pupils. The issue is how such an approach prepares those students for the study of science at a higher level.

The move to teaching science from a process perspective need not mean the 'dumbing down' of science – as has been feared by some (BBC, 2006). The approach advocated, How Science Works, would be the hook on which the subject matter hangs. Using How Science Works and examining how scientists work, how science arrives at explanations and how science influences society will still require the basic and baseline facts of biology, chemistry and physics to be delivered. Consideration of moral and ethical aspects of scientific endeavour cannot be done in a content vacuum.

This chapter started with the aim of exploring what makes science 'science'. To do this we must now move from how science is introduced into our curriculum to consider the key features of the discipline.

Testability and science

As has been stated, testability is a key feature of science. It is part of the primary approach to science – including the well-pressed home idea of 'fair testing'. When considering if an approach to something is scientific we must ask the question 'can my idea be tested?' If an idea can be tested then it passes the first check of whether or not something is science. Our science often starts with a question. For example 'what affects the taste of a strawberry?' This simple question could be investigated scientifically. The question itself will generate many other questions, some of which will be scientific, many others will not.

Take the following questions that a pupil may generate from the initial 'problem' posed:

- Does the type of soil affect the taste?
- Does the amount of ripening affect the taste?
- Does the colour affect the taste?

The first two questions are testable and could be considered as 'scientific' the last question is not testable – other than acknowledging the fact that strawberries, when unripe, are green and not very tasty. We cannot, for example, change the colour of the ripe strawberry significantly. (I accept that shades of red will occur in ripe strawberries and, superficially, it would appear that a test could be set up to look at the taste associated with the various shades of red.) In this problem-solving scenario a scientific investigation could be set up to investigate taste in strawberries. We can reject the 'unscientific' question of colour and taste (we could also reject a question that linked shape to taste). We could show, for example, that chemically there is little to no difference perhaps between strawberries that are different shades of red and so eliminate colour as a factor. Yet psychological studies show us that colour could indeed affect taste, or at least our perception of taste. Often psychologists, and those who conduct taste tests for food manufacturers and producers, will conduct colour neutral tests on food samples, for example bathing them in strong red light to 'fool' the brain and obscure the true colour of the food.

So what do we make of our 'unscientific' question now? Could colour affect taste? In reality, different people will have subtly different palates that affect how they taste various foods. That question, which on first sight appears unscientific, could have a basis in science – in the psychology branch of science.

Testability is one of the underlying principles of science. An inability to test ideas renders that idea unscientific. As can be seen from the above example, depending on the scientific discipline ideas may be scientific in one context (e.g. taste and colour in a psychology context) or unscientific in another (e.g. colour and chemical makeup in a chemistry context).

Popper and falsifiability

The idea of testability in science was used by the philosopher Sir Karl Popper (1902–1994). In thinking about the nature of science and the status of theories, he said:

> 'When should a theory be ranked as scientific?' or 'Is there a criterion for the scientific character or status of a theory?' The problem which troubled me at the time was neither, 'When is a theory true?' nor 'When is a theory acceptable?', my problem was different. I wished to distinguish between science and pseudo-science; knowing very well that science often errs, and that pseudoscience may happen to stumble on the truth. I knew, of course, the most widely accepted answer to my problem: that science is distinguished from pseudoscience – or from 'metaphysics' – by its empirical method, which is essentially inductive, proceeding from observation or experiment. But this did not satisfy me.
>
> (Popper, 2002: 33)

Popper believed in a creative force in scientific thinking and that everyone, including experimental and theoretical scientists, would have a bias. He stated that science advances by 'deductive falsification' through a process of 'conjectures and refutations', the title of his 1963 book. He asserted that if a theory can be shown to be falsifiable then it is scientific; if it cannot then it is pseudoscience. He went on to claim that experiment and observations test theories; they do not necessarily produce them. So testability is still a key feature of science, but according to Popper the testing is about falsification.

Kuhn and 'normal science'

By way of contrast, Thomas Kuhn in his book *The structure of scientific revolutions* (1996) put forward a view of how science proceeds or operates through 'revolutions'. He postulated that competing scientific workers initially generate a number of theoretical standpoints or frameworks, which are in direct competition. Over time, one of these becomes the dominant framework, that is, the one that explains the largest number of phenomena observed. Kuhn called this a durable 'paradigm'. Once this paradigm is accepted and used, during a period that Kuhn calls 'normal science', contradictory observations and accounts test the paradigm, undermining its dominant position. New frameworks are then developed to account for the anomalous observations and eventually a new 'paradigm' is adopted. This is the nature of what Kuhn terms his 'scientific revolution'. What is important here is that the new model or paradigm does not always completely replace the old paradigm and the two may coexist, as with for example, Newtonian physics and Einsteinian physics.

Feyerabend's anarchistic theory of science

Paul Feyerabend (1924–1994) countered the notion of any form of scientific method. In his most famous book, *Against Method* (1975), derived from a 1970 essay of the same title, he set out his argument against the notion of any scientific method. Feyerabend later conceded that he had merely introduced another rigid concept, perhaps even another form of scientific method.

> *One of my motives for writing Against Method was to free people from the tyranny of philosophical obfuscators and abstract concepts such as 'truth', 'reality', or 'objectivity', which narrow people's vision and ways of being in the world. Formulating what I thought were my own attitude and convictions, I unfortunately ended up by introducing concepts of similar rigidity, such as 'democracy', 'tradition', or 'relative truth'. Now that I am aware of it, I wonder how it happened. The urge to explain one's own ideas, not simply, not in a story, but by means of a 'systematic account', is powerful indeed.*
>
> (Feyerabend, 1996: 179–80)

Science, for Feyerabend, is an anarchistic enterprise, his idea being that theoretical anarchism is more humanitarian and more likely to encourage progress than any 'law and order' alternative. This, he believed, was shown both by an examination of historical episodes and by an abstract analysis of the relation between ideas and actions. The only principle that did not inhibit progress for Feyerabend was 'anything goes'.

Whether or not a scientific method exists, has been the subject of debate for many years. The biologist Sir Peter Medawar, who won a Nobel Prize for his work on tissue grafting and tissue rejection paving the way for organ transplants, once said,

> Ask a scientist what he conceives the scientific method to be and he will adopt an expression that is at once solemn and shifty eyed: solemn because he feels that he ought to declare an opinion: shifty because he is wondering how to conceal the fact that he has no opinion to declare.

(Medawar, 1982)

Science in a school-based context

Science, even in a school-based context, has its own language, procedures, equipment and philosophy. How explicit that is in the classroom will depend on the teacher. The discipline of science has for many years been a fact-based discipline. Take, for instance, what constituted studying science in the pre-GCSE examination days at O and A level. Thirty years ago pupils were required to learn the features of major taxa (zoology and botany); it was common for teachers to require their pupils to be able to name the first twenty elements of the periodic table (chemistry O level); learn and repeat the laws of thermodynamics (physics) and recite the geological timescale (geology O and A level). There was less emphasis on understanding and more on rote learning and reproduction of knowledge (diagrams of the eye and ear; biochemical pathways etc.). Since that time the move away from rote learning without understanding has been marked. Does it represent 'dumbing down'? or is the move a recognition that the available body of knowledge that we refer to as science expands to such a great extent that, unlike the philosophers (scientists) of the sixteenth, seventeenth, even eighteenth centuries no one person can now hold the body of knowledge that we call science. In the university system there has been a proliferation of degrees and the introduction of modularity so much so that no A level specification is going to satisfy the basic knowledge requirements of many degree programmes. The move away from fact-based teaching to process-based science seems to be a reasonable one that ultimately should equip pupils with the skills and ability to work scientifically.

We cannot ignore the idea that any subject we are studying will require the learning of some basic facts. Exactly what is taught and learned, what the essential 'basic facts' are needs to be agreed – but by whom? Should the university curriculum drive the teaching in schools or should what is taught in schools be agreed just by teachers? Here is not the place for that debate, but it would be a matter of common sense for professional scientists, academic scientists and science educators to be the people who agree what should be taught. The role of the examination boards should be to examine the agreed curriculum.

Whatever the method of developing the curriculum, the key thing is to agree what those basics are and to provide them not as a discrete package with a claim that this represents what the discipline of science is all about. The 'facts' should come as a result of the process, not, the process as a consequence of the 'facts' being taught in science.

For the purposes of school science we need a workable definition and description that meets the needs of a wide range of pupils, abilities and purposes. We must also be aware that the science we teach in schools, no matter how carefully and how much we try, is not the science we would observe in a real working situation. The science we provide in schools models 'real' science and capitalizes on the exciting, engaging aspects of the subject. What we are trying to develop when teaching school science is explanation, argumentation, process and skills. Students should be able to provide explanation of common scientific phenomena; they should be able to articulate an idea of how science is done (How Science Works) in the working environment and they must develop skills in argumentation and practical skills which enable them to conduct basic experiments and manipulate scientific equipment.

To this end then we can say that science:

- provides explanations of natural phenomena and does not provide explanations of the supernatural;
- is a way of learning about what is in the natural world (universe) and how the natural world (universe) works;
- seeks to explain and describe how the natural world (universe) has changed over time to reach its present state;
- is carried out by scientists who work in many different ways;
- proceeds through argumentation either between scientists or through a process of internal argumentation;
- involves the testing of ideas, but those ideas must be in the form of a scientific question;
- provides explanations (scientific theories) of natural phenomena and that these are accepted as reliable because they have been thoroughly tested;

- will change and modify its theories if and when new evidence supports such a change;
- is a human endeavour.

Children will always press for reasons why we should study science and why it is important. The sort of ideas that teachers, and others, present often state that science:

- can affect human lives on a day-to-day basis in a variety of ways;
- can be used to enable you to live and function in an increasingly technological world;
- is a career that is open to everyone and can be carried out as a professional or as an amateur.

Science and 'The' scientific method

Having discussed what we may consider to be the characteristics of science and considered it in a school setting, the crucial question that remains is *does having a particular way of "doing" science, make something "science"?* In other words, does a scientific method really exist and is this what defines what we call science, is it following a scientific method that makes science 'science'?

As outlined in Chapter 2, science from its early days to the time of Sir Francis Bacon, was mostly deductive in its reasoning. The rules of logic applied and the conclusions from deductive reasoning were valid, or invalid, strong or weak. A strong deductive conclusion can be made when the information or data that supports such a conclusion is, itself valid. With a deductive reasoning approach in science, rather than talking about proof, we should, as science teachers, talk about conclusions being valid or invalid. It is possible to come to an invalid conclusion even if the logic is correct. For example; a bird has wings, a bat has wings, therefore a bat is a bird. The logic may be correct but the conclusion is invalid. It is, of course partly to do with the fact that we have chosen to classify the animal world in such a way that birds and bats belong to different groups.

Science also uses induction as a way of reasoning. Inductive reasoning does not necessarily lead to a valid or invalid conclusion. It is more a case of the probability of the conclusion being more or less valid. The strength of inductive reasoning is in the number of initial supporting instances. This is related to the number of data points or observations made. In science more data, more observations lead to a more reliable conclusion.

Whether a scientist uses deductive and/or inductive reasoning will depend on whether or not the work that they are doing is theory building or theory confirming. With deductive reasoning, a general principle or established theory in science is the initial premise from which a valid conclusion can be inferred. Where scientists are seeking to develop explanations from their observations or data then induction is the method followed. For science and the scientific method then, it is not a case of 'either/or' deduction/induction. Science can, and does, utilize both approaches to establish the validity of an argument or to test the established, prevailing explanations. Chapter 7 explores this issue in more detail.

A scientific method, however, is not just how to reason or use logic to come to answers or explanations. Asking graduate scientists to explain what 'scientific method' means to them elicits some interesting responses (Williams, 2007; Williams, 2008) from a description of 'scientific method' as a way of writing up the outcome of an experiment (hypothesis, method, results, conclusions etc.) through to Popper's ideas on falsifiability.

Conclusion

Neither Bacon, Popper, Kuhn nor Feyerabend provides us with an uncontroversial picture of what science is or, indeed, how it works. By reading their views on science we should be able to gain a deeper understanding.

Scientists are not all Baconian observers; they may 'become Baconian' when they describe their observations in their published work. Scientists are rigorous in how they present and finally publish their work. Data are the currency of science and they are always treated with great regard and respect. Should data have been found to have been improperly generated or reported it rightly shocks the community and brings harsh penalties on those who perpetrate scientific fraud.

Scientists do not have to falsify their own theories; there are many others who will oblige and attempt to falsify a rival's theory. Although Kuhn's notion of scientific revolutions may suggest wholesale step changes in how we view the workings of the world around us, scientific progress is, perhaps, more incremental than revolutionary. The science of the twentieth century has undoubtedly provided more explanation and more detailed understanding of natural phenomena than the explanations for those same phenomena put forward in the eighteenth and seventeenth centuries. It is almost a foregone conclusion that as the twenty-first century progresses so too will our knowledge and understanding progress. The move from Newtonian physics to Einsteinian physics was a revolution, but science and, indeed, the physics textbooks have not thrown out all of Newton's 'laws' and neither should they.

The fundamental question of whether or not there is one agreed 'scientific method' and that this is indeed 'how science works' appears to have no simple answer. Chalmers (1990), in describing the difficulties that science has in either proving or disproving theories states that, '. . . *the reconstructions of philosophers bear little resemblance to what actually goes on in science*' his reaction to this being that we should '*give up altogether the idea that science is a rational activity operating according to some special method or methods*' (Chalmers, 1999: xvii).

Neither Chalmers nor Feyerabend was the first to postulate that the 'scientific method' does not exist. The philosopher Cornelius Benjamin (1897–1968), stated that:

> The strongest grounds for contending that there is no scientific method is the fact that science consists, in the final analysis, of scientific discovery, and that there are no rules by which this act takes place.
>
> (Benjamin, 1956: 234)

So where does an examination of the history and philosophy of science leave us in relation to school science and meeting the needs of the new key stage 4 programme of study based on the notion of HSW? In generating the new specifications for GCSE sciences, all examination bodies moved from a content-based approach to a process-based approach that was determined by HSW. It would be reasonable to assume that this followed some agreed definition of how science works or that scientists, due to the nature of their studies in scientific disciplines, would have a common approach. In addition, definitions of common terms used in science should also have a degree of commonality and consistency (see Chapter 4). Such assumptions would be incorrect.

Reflective task

Think about the attributes of science which help us define in practical terms what we teach day to day in the classroom. Simply looking at science as a body of knowledge, for example in biology and defining science in terms of that body of knowledge would be restrictive and perhaps may exclude what we traditionally think of as scientific. Come to a definition of science that encompasses your ideas of what science is and which will serve as a definition for your pupils and colleagues.

Classroom task

Astronomy and astrology are two completely different things which some people confuse. Astronomy is a science and astrology is not science. Think about why astronomy is a science – what makes the study of the stars scientific. What makes fortune telling and trying to read your future from the position of the stars not scientific?

Think about how you can devise a test to show that astrology is not scientific and does not really predict the future. How could you make your test 'scientific'?

References

BBC, 2006. *Critics Attack New Science GCSE* [Online]. London: BBC News. Available: http://news.bbc.co.uk/1/hi/education/6038638.stm [Accessed 12 November 2009/ 2010].

Benjamin, A. C. 1956. Is there a scientific method? *The Journal of Higher Education*, Vol. 27, No. 5 (May 1956) pp. 233–238.

Braund, M. and Hames, V. 2005. Improving progression and continuity from primary to secondary science: pupils' reactions to bridging work. *International Journal of Science Education*, 27, 781–801.

Chalmers, A. F. 1999. *What Is This Thing Called Science?* Milton Keynes: Open University Press.

Feyerabend, P. 1996. *Killing Time: The Autobiography of Paul Feyerabend*, Chicago: Chicago University Press.

Feyerabend, P. K. 1975. *Against Method*, London:Verso.

Kuhn, T. S. 1996. *The Structure of Scientific Revolutions*, Chicago: University of Chicago Press.

Medawar, P. 1982. *Pluto's Republic*, Oxford: Oxford University Press.

Popper, K. 2002. *Conjectures and Refutations: The Growth of Scientific Knowledge,* London: Routledge.

Thompson, D. (ed.) 1995. *The Concise Oxford Dictionary,* Oxford: Oxford University Press.

Williams, J. D. 2007. Just How Does Science Work: the scientific method and key stage 4 science. In: Burton, N., ed. ATSE Annual Conference: Resourcing Initial Teacher Training, 2007 Newport, South Wales. Association for Science Education, 61–80.

Williams, J. D. 2008. The scientific method and school science. *Journal of College Science Teachers.*

4 Laws, Facts, Theories and Hypotheses

'When I use a word,' Humpty Dumpty said, in rather a scornful tone, 'it means just what I choose it to mean – neither more nor less.' 'The question is,' said Alice, 'whether you can make words mean so many different things.'

(Alice in Wonderland)

Teachers of English or modern foreign languages are adept at dealing with language. It is, after all, their prime focus. Try teaching English without looking at language and meaning or try teaching children how to communicate in a second language without reference to words, translations and their meanings and you will be hard pushed, if not completely defeated. Often, language teachers will look at the roots of words and discuss the similarities of modern European words which have their roots in Latin or Greek. The etymology of most scientific terms has a basis in Latin and/or Greek. The prefixes, suffixes and roots of words, when understood in terms of Latin and Greek serve to demystify science. Lessons in science should include aspects of language teaching if we are to make sense of science for our pupils. Simply teaching children that the suffix '– itis' just means 'inflammation' suddenly makes a range of medical terminology so much easier to understand.

The language of science is something that permeates the work of science teachers. Words in science sometimes have multiple meanings – for example a cell in biology versus the cell in physics. In addition, often there are vernacular meanings for many words as opposed to the scientific meaning. A conductor in science could be a material that transmits electricity or heat. In everyday life it could be a person who directs an orchestra or (increasingly rarely) collects money on a bus. The context within which the word is used provides subtle, yet important clues as to which meaning we must apply. Context, however, is not the be all and end all. Mistakes may still happen. Take the following simple sentence: 'Copper is a good conductor'. This seems to be unambiguous. The metal copper is, indeed, a good conductor (of heat and electricity). In the United States of America, there is a musician by the name of Andrew Copper. He is a performer of chamber music who holds a degree in performance and he plays the French Horn. He is likely to be a good conductor of chamber music. On two levels then, this sentence works – for the metal and for the musician. Given a wider context, for example the sentence as spoken by a science teacher in a science lesson looking at the properties of metals, there is no doubt about the meaning of the word conductor. Saying the sentence in an everyday setting does not preclude the musical meaning. This may be an extreme example of the issue of scientific meaning over vernacular meaning, but it becomes more important when we consider how 'scientific' words are used in everyday life. Some words, such as mass and weight have everyday meanings that are different from strict scientific meanings (mass being the amount of matter and weight being mass and the effect of gravity on that mass). We are used to casually misusing words in science in an everyday context and we also sometimes abuse the use of units for everyday use (e.g. mass and weight again).

Some words are troublesome – such as energy – for other reasons, in that their use can reinforce scientific misconceptions. It is common for pupils and adults to misuse the word energy referring to it as if it was a substance or tangible thing. Teaching children (even adults) to appreciate the subtly of meaning in science can be quite difficult. Even terminology which appears to be uncomplicated – such as theory and law are not free from misuse and misunderstanding.

Facts and science

The word fact is derived from the Latin term *factum* which means an 'act' or 'deed'. Its use over time has changed the meaning from the original and often the term is used synonymously with 'true' or 'real'. In science we talk sometimes about 'gathering facts' when perhaps what we mean is gathering data. We can also state that something is a 'fact' when we really are saying that something has been accepted by the scientific community, not that something is 'true'. If we look up the dictionary definition of 'fact' we find more than one meaning.

> Fact (n) 1. A thing that is known to have occurred, to exist or be true 2. A datum of experience 3. An item of verified information; a piece of evidence 4. Truth, reality 5. A thing assumed as the basis for argument or inference.
>
> (Thompson, 1995: 482)

The everyday meaning of fact often resides in the realms of definitions 1 and 4 – when people are asked what a fact is, they will often refer to the idea of truth or something that is 'known' (Williams, 2008). For the purposes of science, a fact really resides in definitions 2 and 3. I would suggest that to eliminate any potential misunderstanding of the word 'fact', it should, when used in a scientific sense, have the adjective 'scientific' attached to modify the noun and ensure that the meaning is clear. This term, 'scientific fact' can then be defined in such a way as to eliminate undesirable attachments such as 'truth'.

Scientific facts are independent of the scientist who is observing or measuring them. The idea is that the scientific fact remains unchanged, whoever is measuring or observing it. The result of the observation or measurement should be consistent that is the observers should agree on what it was they were seeing or observing and the measurements should be the same (here I am not specifying that the measurements should be **exactly** the same as it would depend on the degree of precision used when measuring – see page 114 for a definition of precision).

Linking the definition of a 'fact' with truth and reality in science is problematic. As we saw in Chapter 1, the nature of science means that science is provisional and subject to change. The 'fact' that mountains and continents could not move apart needed to be revised and changed when plate tectonics provided a mechanism whereby such seemingly impossible things could happen. Facts, then, in science may be subject to change. This is at odds with definitions of facts as truth or reality. Truth does not change and reality should not be subject to change. The addition of 'scientific' to fact helps preserve its status in science as different from that in law or everyday experience.

The hypothesis in science

The hypothesis in science is often the starting point for an explanation of observed phenomena or scientific facts. The word derives from the Greek and Late Latin term *hypothesis* and means *'the basis of an argument or proposition'* – *hypo* – meaning 'under' and *thesis* meaning 'a proposition'. In practice a hypothesis is an informed guess at an explanation for observed phenomena. It is not a wild guess or mere speculation – the hypothesis must also be able to be tested to see if it is correct or not. Any hypothesis that cannot be tested is not, strictly speaking, scientific.

The term hypothesis is often used interchangeably with theory by laypeople and scientists alike. To avoid confusion, teachers (and for that matter professional scientists) should not say hypothesis when they mean theory and theory when they mean hypothesis. This just adds to the problem of language in science and the precise use of language to ensure accuracy of meaning. Theories in science (see below) are another form of explanation in science, they may still be tested but they have a much wider acceptance as being valid explanations of observations of phenomena.

Another problem with the term hypothesis is that as we progress in science (often within biological sciences) teachers bring into use the 'null hypothesis' – the opposite of the hypothesis. When hypothesis is used in conjunction with 'null hypothesis', most often during A level biology teaching, it can also be referred to as the 'alternative' or 'research' hypothesis. The use of 'alternative and null hypothesis' is statistical in origin and should not be confused with the scientific use of the term hypothesis. The following example will serve to illustrate the difference between statistical hypothesis and scientific hypothesis.

A chemist producing a drug that deals with high blood pressure may wish to run a trial to see the effect of the drug in the mainstream population (given that the drug had passed all the hurdles of being allowed to be tested on humans). The alternative or research hypothesis would be that use of the drug will reduce high blood pressure in patients. The null hypothesis would be that use of the drug has no effect on high blood pressure. As hypotheses go, this is testable. You simply find a sample of people with high blood pressure, administer the drug over a period of time then monitor blood pressure and see if the high blood pressure previously recorded is lowered. If the finding is that blood pressure is reduced then the alternative hypothesis is correct, otherwise it is the null hypothesis that has been verified. This is, of course, a very simplistic description of a clinical trials procedure that would be very much more complex and involved in real life. What is being tested here is not a scientific hypothesis but a statistical hypothesis. The outcome of the 'test' or trial is determined by statistical analyses of the results. The trial will not provide an explanation of how the drug lowers blood pressure, just that statistically it does (or does not) work.

We must be careful to distinguish the scientific hypothesis from the statistical hypothesis. Very commonly in biology, statistical hypotheses are used to determine general patterns in observations or data. Scientific hypotheses explain these patterns, often with reference to underlying mechanisms.

Hypotheses and predictions

Part of the process of scientific hypothesis testing is prediction. Students are encouraged to make predictions about what they think will happen when they investigate some phenomena or another. They are encouraged to write down what they think will happen (the prediction) and why they think something will happen (hypothesis). There is a danger that the prediction is seen as part, if not all, of the hypothesis. Predictions can be confirmed or not through observation and measurement, rather than testing, which separates them from hypotheses as these require some form of test.

Predictions may be simple or require complex sophisticated observations/ measurements. A simple prediction may be that if a rubber ball is dropped it will bounce. This prediction is easily verified (or not) – drop a rubber ball and see if it bounces. You need only to observe the ball and not even measure the bounce to see if the prediction is correct. Consider the statement '*dropping a rubber ball at increasing heights above the ground makes the ball bounce higher*'

Is this a prediction or a hypothesis? Again, this is something that can be verified by observation alone. Dropping the ball at intervals of 0.5, 1.0 and 1.5m above the laboratory floor, it will be easy to see if it bounces higher the greater the height from which it is dropped. As such, what sounded like a hypothesis (which many students will have stated is such in investigations at primary and secondary level), is in fact just a prediction. To turn the statement into a hypothesis, a testable idea would have to be developed to involve more things (factors), such as the surface, the type of ball etc. The sign that the hypothesis has been tested and an explanation found to explain any observations (such as a rubber ball bounces to different heights on different surfaces) would then perhaps have to contain some reference to what makes the ball bouncy in the first place as well as controlling factors to enable a 'fair test'.

The notion that hypotheses are scientific if they can be tested and falsified holds with predictions as well. Simply using testability and falsifiability as the guardian of science is not enough since this does not help us differentiate between a scientific hypothesis and a mere prediction. The formulation and testing of hypotheses is central to any scientific method. Distinguishing between hypothesis generation and prediction is at best rudimentary in school science, with many professional scientists not cognizant of the difference (McPherson, 2001).

In teaching How Science Works we must ensure that our pupils understand in general terms what a scientific hypothesis is and how this differs from a prediction. Seeing and recognizing patterns is important in science and often we will use statistical hypotheses to test our ideas of whether or not these patterns exist and if they are significant. At the heart of science is explanation. The accepted explanations of science that result from scientific hypothesis testing are theories.

Theories and science

Scientific knowledge is provisional; it is in a state of change. As new observations and evidence come to light, scientific knowledge and understanding is always being refined and revised. For some this is seen as a weakness. Surely science should present unchanging explanations and definitive answers? For students science is often a matter of right or wrong, black or white. That science can be 'grey', a bit right and a bit wrong, with tentative answers and explanations, poses problems. The issue is partly down to how people perceive science; as a way of knowing the 'truth' and as a way of explaining everything. Perhaps as science teachers the approach of teaching science, as a series of 'facts' which need to be learned and as experiments where the 'right' answer can be found, is at the heart of the problem. Add to this a popular view of science as a means of making the 'unknown' 'known' with popular news stories proclaiming that 'science' has discovered the cure to a disease or found answers to long-held mysteries, science as 'the' authority becomes the accepted vision.

A remarkable feature of science is that many of its well-known explanations of phenomena are relatively stable. Even though all science is provisional, many common explanations in science have held up to intense scrutiny over many years, in some cases hundreds of years. Those accepted, well-evidenced explanations we call theories. Unlike a vernacular use of the word, a scientific theory is not a speculative hunch or guess. To attain the status of 'theory' in science requires that certain conditions are met. Scientific theories must be: useful, testable, consistent, economical, correctable, verifiable and progressive.

Useful theories: when explaining any observations the theory must have use. From the theory you should be able to make predictions. Those predictions are themselves a useful test of the theory. If the predictions are correct it strengthens the theory. If the predictions are incorrect they weaken the theory. Scientific theories should also be able to explain a wide range of observations.

Testable theories: as with scientific hypotheses, a scientific theory must be testable and falsifiable. Even though a scientific theory is the pinnacle of scientific explanation and it is scientific theory that underpins the whole of science, it does not make the explanation immune from testing. Despite ideas to the contrary, accepted scientific theories are not protected from testing and, should they be shown to be wrong or deficient, the theory is open to change, revision and refinement. It is also open to complete abandonment.

Consistent theories: explanations that come with multiple caveats and exceptions are inherently weak as scientific theories. In addition, a scientific theory should be able to explain a wide series of observations. It should be widely applicable to the phenomenon.

Economical theories: the best scientific theories are often the simplest. They are economical in explanation. A long, involved, complex explanation that requires a high degree of knowledge or understanding or that requires a high degree of learning makes the scientific theory less easy to assimilate.

Correctable theories: any scientific theory that is not open to correction is not a theory but a dogma. Even the best scientific theories will be open to correction as our knowledge and understanding increases, as our observations increase in number, and as our predictions are confirmed or refuted. Even long-standing theories, for example the theory of evolution by means of natural selection, first proposed in 1858, has been subject to many tests and millions of observations. Over time it has been subject to corrections as our knowledge and understanding of evolution increases.

Verifiable theories: a scientific theory that cannot be verified cannot be scientific. Popper stated that true scientific theories are never fully verified, for example a classic argument about verification rests on whether all swans are white. It is impossible to verify such a 'theory' in that you would have to have looked at every swan living, every swan that has ever lived and every swan that will ever live in order to fully verify the statement and that is clearly impossible. But theories can be verified by the predictions and retro-dictions that you can make. Retro-dictions (extrapolations into the past) can be made for evolution theory, many of which have held up to scientific investigation. Looking at the evolutionary line of a particular group of animals there are often gaps in the fossil record. This is not surprising given the rarity of the fossilization process and the likelihood of any individual animal being fossilized. A retro-diction in the fossil record would be the extrapolation from current or more recent fossils to ancestral forms. When such fossilized forms are found it acts as a verification of evolution theory. Charles Darwin, for example, held the view that sea mammals evolved from land-based animals. His progression went from land-based mammals to those who lived in fresh-water environments with legs that were not fully developed into flippers, to marine creatures with flippers. A retro-diction of this would be that in the fos-sil record a creature will be found that shows transitional features between a land-based animal and a fully marine seal-like animal. In 2009 a fossil, named *Pujilla darwini* , in Darwin's honour, was discovered in Canada which filled one gap (Black, 2009). This is just one small example of a verification of evolution theory.

Tentative theories: as has been stated, all scientific theories are tentative or provisional. No scientific theory is truly thought of as correct. Some, such as gravity or evolution have such a weight of evidence that to think of them as anything other than correct would be in some ways perverse. Science, however, does not preclude the possibility that the theory of evolution as now understood could be wrong and that the mechanism of evolution, natural selection, is not the only dominant mechanism. If we consider gravity, for example, it may act differently is some part of the universe from the way that gravitation theory is described by us today on earth.

In short science is willing to admit that its theories might not be correct. This important feature sets science apart from dogma and faith-based positions. It separates science from religion, an important factor for some areas of science that deal with difficult issues such as life's origins and development.

Laws, principles and science

Scientific laws provide another obstacle for understanding How Science Works for students (and the general population sometimes). Scientific laws, sometimes referred to as physical laws are also Principles. They are inherently different from theories and do not represent a hierarchy in science that leads from hypotheses to theories to principles then laws. Many laws have the status of a law due to its age and the 'conferment' of such a status by the scientist or natural philosopher who first described the principle or law or it is conferred in honour of the scientist/discoverer. Some laws are very familiar to the general public for example Newton's laws of motion. Others, such as Boyle's law, which describes the relationship between pressure and volume of a gas in a closed system, have posed problems for generations of children when asked about in public examinations.

For many, biology does not have laws in the same sense as the physical sciences (Mitchell, 2000). Biologists do talk of Mendel's laws, for example with respect to each pair of alleles at a locus on the chromosome of a sexual organism, 50 per cent of the organism's gametes will carry one representative of that pair, and 50 per cent will carry the other representative of the pair. This is often known as Mendel's first law or the law of segregation. His second law is the law of independent assortment. But there are few laws in biology when compared with the physical sciences.

Many of the laws in the physical sciences are named after their discoverers, such as Newton's laws, Hooke's law, Mendel's laws. One of the characteristics of these laws is their empirical nature. Such empirical laws are not restricted to science. Other disciplines, such as linguistics and computing, have their own empirical laws. Zipf's law, named after the linguist George Kingsley Zipf, states that the frequency of any word is inversely proportional to its rank in a frequency table of all the words in use. The most frequent word will occur approximately twice as often as the second most frequent word, which occurs twice as often as the third most frequent word etc. Moore's law, in the field of computing, stated that the number of transistors on an integrated circuit doubles approximately every 2 years. This law first described by the founder of Intel, Gordon Moore in 1965, has since been taken and applied to many other situations, for example computing power; pixels per unit cost in digital cameras etc.

Physical laws in science share certain properties; some of those properties are that:

- they are unchanged since first described (though some have been refined)
- there have never been any repeatable contradicting observations
- they appear to apply everywhere, that is they are universal
- they are often simple and can be expressed in relatively simple mathematical equations.

Once more, it is important to differentiate between those laws which apply to science and other laws – even if they are empirical in nature – so that children are clear of the nature of laws in science. For this reason, as with facts, hypotheses and theories use of the adjective 'scientific' serves to clarify the context within which the term law is being used.

Conclusion

The relationship between facts, hypotheses, theories, laws and principles in science is a complex one that has evolved over hundreds of years. There is no hierarchy that begins with facts and leads to a law. There is a fundamental difference between theories and laws. Theories explain while laws describe. The difference between theories and hypotheses is much less distinct, perhaps the reason why so many scientists and others use the terms interchangeably. This should be avoided and discouraged. To refer to a testable idea as a hypothesis in one breadth and a theory in another will only serve to confuse the general public and students alike.

It may well be that different disciplines in science have subtly different definitions of the key terminology outlined in this chapter. Theoretical physicists, philosophers of science will, no doubt, disagree with aspects of the content of this chapter, but ultimately to make science work in a school situation we must have a common language, agreed terminology and an approach to teaching How Science Works that delivers scientific literacy. The nuances of language as used in different professional scientific disciplines by working scientists can be left until later in a person's education. Provided we teach our pupils that when Inspector Lewis investigates the latest murder in the rolling countryside of Oxfordshire to declare that he has a theory about who did it, they understand that this is not on the same footing as atomic theory, evolution theory or theories of gravity, then that will lead to better scientific literacy. It is for this reason that I advocate the use of the prefix 'scientific' to distinguish the common form of key scientific terminology from the specific use and definition.

Reflective task

1. Scientific terminology can be confusing for children. Many words in science will have a common or vernacular meaning and a precise scientific one. From everyday words such as cell, conductor etc. we must carefully differentiate between common meanings and specific ones. Over the course of a term, gather examples of words that can be confused – write into your schemes of work specific objectives to make clear the distinction between common and specific scientific meanings for words and develop a science literacy policy (as distinct from Scientific Literacy) that addresses the use of language.

2. Discuss the meaning of the terms in the chapter and decide on how such words will be introduced to pupils. Devise a policy for example by requesting that certain terms have the prefix 'scientific' and adjust teaching resources over time to reflect this policy.

Classroom task

Discuss the meaning of key HSW terminology related to 'scientific method'. Determine the pupils' understanding of these words. Then ask them for examples of the words as used in the media, books and comics or on TV (if possible collect some examples from newspapers of the use of the word in the vernacular and specific). For homework a class could look at news reports and newspaper stories on science and pick out where these terms are used. For example, in crime drama does the investigating policeman talk about his theory of how a person was murdered?

References

Black, R. 2009. '*Missing link' Fossil Seal Walked* [Online]. BBC. Available: http://news.bbc.co.uk/1/hi/sci/tech/8012322.stm [Accessed 21 March 2010].

McPherson, G. R. 2001. Teaching & learning the scientific method. *The American Biology Teacher*, 63, 242–245.

Mitchell, S. D. 2000. Dimensions of scientific law. *Philosophy of Science*, 67, 242–265.

Thompson, D. (ed.) 1995. *The Concise Oxford Dictionary*, Oxford: Oxford University Press.

Williams, J. D. 2008. The scientific method and school science. *Journal of College Science Teachers*.

5 Questions and Critical Thinking in Science

The question of questions for mankind . . . is the ascertainment of the place which Man occupies in nature and his relation to the universe of things.

(T. H. Huxley (1825–1895) biologist)

All teachers who have constructed tests and examinations will know that answering questions is a lot easier than asking good questions. Whether you are a researcher or an examiner, the art of good question construction is something that has to be learned. Asking good scientific questions also requires knowledge and understanding, not just of how to create them, but also of what the science is and how science works. Developing a good scientific question is part of the process of hypothesizing. Good scientific questions are those that can be answered by observation or through the use of scientific-related tools. In this chapter we will look at the anatomy of scientific questions, consider other categories of questions and consider how this leads on to the development of critical thinking skills.

The characteristics of a scientific question

Questions that are scientific in nature are, for the most part, untested hypotheses. Logically therefore, what makes a good hypothesis is a statement, which may be posed in the form of a question, that can be put to the test. There are four main characteristics that can be applied to the description of a good scientific question.

    1. A good scientific question can be answered through scientific research or experimentation:

'Do heavier things fall faster than lighter things' is, superficially, a good question because you should be able to provide a prediction, devise a way of testing your idea and discover if heavier things fall faster than lighter ones. Even this question however has inherent problems when it comes to the design of the experiment. Comparing two stainless steel ball bearings of differing size and mass poses few problems, but comparing a feather with a steel ball bearing will, as you will readily realize, have implications for the experimental design and the control of key variables. This, in itself, does not make the question a bad one or non-scientific. It simply reflects the problem that science always has to deal with – variables.

    2. Good scientific questions often build on what is already known (partially or fully) and on what you can find out.

Much of science does not involve entirely new ideas, concepts or knowledge. In school science, the topics under investigation certainly will not be new and will not involve new (to science) ideas, concepts and processes. This being the case, there will be a body of knowledge about the ideas, concepts and processes that we teach about. Background research will provide additional information on which the students can build. Often, such background research will help define new questions. The background information will necessarily provide ideas on how to investigate the new question and it is important for teachers to provide students with the justification for such background research and knowledge. In one sense it is the application of new knowledge and understanding (for the students) in different contexts which develops understanding. This is also a higher-level thinking skill which we seek to develop in our students.

3. Good scientific questions can be tested by experiment.

The nature of scientific 'experiments' and the associated language is discussed more fully in Chapter 9. Essentially scientific experiments can consist of observing, measuring or obtaining data in a real situation, for example measuring the products from a reaction, to running a scientific model (e.g. a computer simulation) and analysing the results of changing key variables. The result of any experiment will be data and these data must be analysed. A good scientific question will enable data to be collected that can be synthesized, analysed, described and presented (sometimes graphically, sometimes as a written narrative).

4. A good scientific question often prompts other good questions.

A wonderful and interesting aspect of science is that there are few questions, which, in turn, do not lead to other good questions. Experiments or investigations which produce more questions than answers should be seen as a positive characteristic of science and not a problem or an issue. Even simple investigations, such as looking at the pollution of a local pond can lead to questions such as 'what is the source of the pollution?' or 'how does the pollution affect different plant and animal populations?'

Developing skills in question asking

Being able to devise interesting, pertinent and good scientific questions does not come easily to students. As with all skills, students need practice in devising questions and a model on which to base their ideas. A first step would be to look at existing questions and identify those which are scientific and those which are not.

Take the example of investigating the taste of foods, a series of questions can be constructed:

- Does the soil in which carrots are grown affect the taste of the carrot?
- Does the age of a carrot affect its taste?
- How does the colour of a carrot affect its taste?
- Does the size of a carrot affect the taste?
- Do organically grown carrots differ in taste from non-organically grown carrots?

Each of the above questions will, at first glance, be testable in some way. We can grow carrots in different soils and eat them. We can compare different varieties of carrot that have different colours (including purple carrots) etc. The problem we very quickly encounter is that what we are trying to measure is taste. Different people will have different ideas about what is a 'good' taste. Some people just will not like carrots and will not be willing to score the taste very highly. So overall, while the questions may have scientifically testable elements to them, ultimately the variable which we are trying to measure, taste, is more a matter of opinion than something that can easily be objectively measured. The final question begins to enter the arena of moral/ethical questions which will confuse matters even more. Scientific evidence from studies appears to show that there is no difference in organically grown foods over those produced in a non-organic way. The debates over organic versus non-organic foods do sometimes centre on taste, yet experiments where people who claim to be able to differentiate between organic and non-organic foods by taste show that this is not the case. So a question such as 'are organic foods better than inorganic foods?' could be seen as a loaded question which could cover things such as taste, environmental concerns, cost to the farmer/consumer etc. Most of these would not be scientific questions, but the issue of environmental impact of organic over non-organic foods can be scientifically investigated (e.g. effect of chemical fertilizers on the soil, other plant life, associated wildlife, pollution of groundwater, rivers, streams etc). Whether we should buy organic or non-organic foodstuffs enters the territory of moral and ethical arguments/questions.

In Chapter 8 we will look at the moral and ethical dimension in more detail, but we must not forget that in the new regime of How Science Works, there is a moral and ethical dimension to science that needs to be addressed. The issue here is not to confuse and conflate questions of science with questions of morals and ethics unless there is a specific teaching objective to be gained in doing so. Even then, the component parts should be clearly identified as scientific, moral or ethical. This increases the need for us to ensure that students can separate out scientific questions from non-scientific questions and understand the moral and ethical dimensions of science.

Returning to our example of measuring taste, if we were to simply change the variable to something that could be measured, for example if we were conducting experiments on strawberries then we could measure the amount of sugar in strawberries grown under different conditions. This, in turn, may lead us to an opinion that some strawberries, with high sugar contents, are more likely to taste better than those with very low sugar contents. It is still opinion, but the sugar content as determined by scientific analysis would still provide an answer to a question that we can call a scientific question.

Science is often driven by the curiosity scientists have about the world in which they live and the universe that we occupy. Investigation and experimentation to satisfy that curiosity will involve the use of a logical method. Scientific investigation often begins with general questions, from which the scientist will make observations, gather data and conduct experiments. Inevitably, further questions arise which will require investigation, research and experimentation. If the scientist can ask good questions, then the answers to these often accumulate to provide explanations of what he or she is investigating.

- Good questions result in improved understanding.
- Reasonable questions can generate information but there will be little to no improved understanding.
- Poor questions generate poor or misleading information.

At the heart of scientific endeavour is the notion of hypothesis testing and prediction. Good hypotheses will resist attempts to disprove them and they will, in turn, generate more questions which are testable. A hypothesis whose predictions cannot be verified or which is refuted by investigation or experimentation is rejected. In some ways this is a mechanism for judging the quality of the question in scientific terms.

- If the question generated is a way of testing the prediction(s) of a valid hypothesis, it is most likely to be a good question.
- If a question is unconnected with a hypothesis or does not enable you to test prediction(s) it is most likely that the question is a bad question.

Types of questions

Good scientific questions will not arise by chance. Students need to understand the basic anatomy of a good question and they must be able to distinguish different types of questions. Students also need to be able to discuss with each other the questions that they are formulating. By providing them with the characteristics of different question types they will be able to better differentiate what is a scientific question and what is not. Table 5.1 provides an outline of the main question categories.

Table 5.1 Question categories and characteristics

Question Type	Question Characteristics
Scientific	The question is a testable one that asks about phenomena or processes that happen in the natural world. The answer can realistically be found by experimentation or investigation and will allow for the collection and measurement of empirical data.
	Example: How does the heart function in a mammal?
Religious	The question will involve beliefs and practices that are associated with one or other of the recognized religions.
	Example: What does my religion state or prescribe about organ and tissue transplants?
Cultural	The question will often involve behavioural aspects, often religious aspects tend to become interwoven with cultural questions:
	Example: Should traditional organ music be replaced by rock bands to encourage more young people to attend church?
Legal	Legal questions are framed in what is 'right' or 'wrong', but they are based on the norms of a particular society and may or may not have an ethical dimension. The 'correct' answer to such questions may change according to the set of laws that exist in the place where the question is asked. The legally acceptable answer may not be ethically or morally acceptable to some.
	Example: Is the execution of a convicted murderer acceptable?
Moral/Ethical	Moral and ethical questions are about determining right or wrong. These questions are characterized by the words 'could' and 'should'. Some ethical questions are combined with religious/cultural questions as the religious or cultural view may determine the ethical response to a question.
	Moral/ethical questions can often result from conflict between different cultural/religious groups or simply between groups and individuals with different values. Ethical questions can result in judgements about responsibilities, rights, duties, values and principles.
	Example: Should people whose religion forbids blood transfusion have their views ignored by doctors treating patients?

Questioning in science

Learners will, when they are engaged and interested, ask questions of the teacher. More able students can ask questions that increase the depth of their understanding and the interest that they hold in a subject. Less able students tend to ask more direct questions that are about knowledge acquisition rather than deeper understanding. The nature of these questions can also be helpful in guiding students towards effective questioning. Discussion is also a powerful tool in teaching and learning (see Chapter 7). Research on the role and value of scaffolding student discussions in advancing students' ability to co-construct theories and models from data they have collected has shown that engaging students in reasoning practices in science, offering explicit guidance on the roles students can assume to monitor their own and their peers' thinking and fostering a view of science as a process of revision revealed changes in students' conceptual understanding, as well as changes in their beliefs about the nature of scientific problem solving (Herrenkohl et al., 1999).

Too often in science lessons we ask students to do things without asking the simple question – 'who has taught them how to do it?' Those things may be as simple as 'discuss with your neighbour'; 'work in groups' etc., yet how do we know that students 'know' what is entailed in group work, or how to have meaningful discussions? Why then should we assume that students 'know' how to formulate scientific questions? It is here that the scaffolding becomes important.

Assuming that we can teach students how to formulate scientific questions, on their own such questions have limited use. The next step in the process must be gathering data in a bid to answer the questions. The process of science is not so simple that answers will be immediately apparent. What is done with the data/evidence gathered – analysis and synthesis – is important and this is where critical thinking comes into the process of science.

Critical thinking in science

Allied to the notion of questions in science is critical thinking. Even if our students are able to produce good scientific questions, they will, at the point of analysing and evaluating evidence, need to apply critical thinking skills. Critical thinking is about the pursuit of relevant and reliable knowledge of the natural world. Having formulated a good scientific question, the resultant investigation or experimentation should provide evidence which needs to be subject to critical thinking in order to establish its relevance and reliability. Critical thinking within science should result in the investigator or experimenter deciding what evidence to accept and what to reject. Critical thinkers can ask appropriate questions (i.e. those that follow on from the original scientific question); are able to gather relevant information, rather than simply gather all the available evidence; can apply reasoning to the evidence gathered as well as create logical arguments which deliver conclusions that are robust and reliable.

Exactly what constitutes critical thinking in science education is not universally accepted or understood. Bailin (2002) challenges the assumption that critical thinking is just a set of processes or skills. She claims that conceiving of critical thinking as including things such as formulating questions, seeking answers, analysis, interpretation, problem solving, decision-making and communication, may not always be helpful. Instead she argues that we should shift from thinking about critical thinking as the application of processes and the acquisition of skills to the question of what one needs to understand in order to meet the criteria of good thinking in particular contexts. Critical thinking, she argues,

> always takes place in response to a particular task, question, problematic situation or challenge, including solving problems, evaluating theories, conducting inquiries, interpreting works, and engaging in creative tasks and such challenges always arise in particular contexts. Dealing with these challenges in a critical way involves drawing on a complex array of understandings (what colleagues and I have termed intellectual resources), the particular resources needed for any challenge depending on the specific context.
>
> (Bailin, 2002: 368)

Whichever conception of critical thinking you agree with or practise, either as processes and skills or as criteria – what Bailin calls 'intellectual resources' and processes applied in particular contexts, students are not born with the power to think critically. Critical thinking has to be taught and we must also acknowledge that some students will not learn how to think critically.

Delivering science from the perspective of How Science Works should provide greater opportunities for teachers to deliver critical thinking processes, skills and criteria. In some ways the process of critical thinking, insofar as it can be identified as a process, mimics the approach that science takes: a question is identified; a hypothesis formulated; relevant data sought and gathered; the hypothesis is logically tested and evaluated and reliable conclusions are drawn.

It could be argued that critical thinking is scientific thinking. Ideally a goal of science education is the cultivation of critical thinking. It is useful therefore to think about the characteristics of a critical thinker. In general these characteristics will (but not exclusively) include:

- skilful and impartial use of evidence
- concise and coherent organization and articulation of thoughts
- an ability to distinguish between valid and invalid inferences in logical arguments
- an understanding of the difference between reasoning and rationalizing
- an ability to see similarities and analogies that are not immediately apparent
- independent learning
- an ability to use problem-solving techniques in new and novel areas
- an ability to present verbal arguments free of irrelevant information
- self-reflection
- an awareness of the limitations of current understanding

Critical thinking and How Science Works

Science is often identified as a good place to develop and teach critical thinking because of the relationship between scientific thinking and critical thinking as articulated above. Scientists must be good critical thinkers and therefore it is easy to assume that science teachers will themselves be good critical thinkers capable of teaching critical thinking. A potential flaw in this seemingly logical argument is that many science teachers have never engaged with the history and philosophy of science and are themselves not necessarily fully understanding of the nature of science and any form of 'scientific method'. This is due to their own education in science which has been focused on the facts of science rather than the process of science, or How Science Works (Williams, 2007a; Williams, 2007b; Williams, 2008).

A research summary on critical thinking 25 years ago provides some interesting highlights, as summarized by Norris (1985), all of which could still apply today:

- **Critical thinking is a complex of many considerations**
  It requires individuals to assess their own views and the views of others, to seek alternatives and make inferences as well as having the disposition to think critically
- **Critical thinking is an educational ideal**
  Students have a moral right to be taught how to think critically
- **Critical thinking ability is not widespread**
  Most students do not score well on critical thinking tests, adults also can make simple judgemental errors on simple problems
- **Critical thinking is sensitive to context**
  Students' backgrounds, knowledge and assumptions can affect their ability to make correct inferences.
- **Critical thinking requires knowledge**
  Problem solving cannot happen in the absence of knowledge
- **Teachers should examine the reasoning behind students' conclusions**
  A correct answer may not be the result of critical thinking – extended writing or talking is needed to explore if critical thinking processes and skills are involved in determining the correct answer

It is this last characteristic that is most important in the classroom. As indicated, sometimes students will provide the 'correct' answer, yet demonstrate very little understanding of why the answer is correct. If you look at Bloom's taxonomy and the cognitive domain (see page 106), the lowest level of questioning that we operate in the classroom is simple knowledge restatement. 'What is the chemical symbol for Silver?' 'How many body sections and legs does a typical insect have?' 'What is the equation for calculating speed?' 'What type of rock is sandstone?' In all these cases a pupil may know (or not know) the correct answer, but how much that tells us about what they **understand** about the construction of the periodic table, the rock cycle, taxonomy or the relationship between distance and time is very questionable.

In this respect, critical thinking is not just about extending a student's knowledge, but exploring and enabling them to gain a deeper understanding of the work they are doing. By examining the reason behind a student's answer we can explore their ability to think critically, to analyse and synthesize and we can gain a deeper understanding ourselves of how a student is progressing. It can be said that 'why' is the watchword of science, scientists ask why all the time. Science teachers should also be asking 'why' but not of the science, of the student; 'why do you think that the answer is X?'

Conclusion

Developing the ability to ask scientific questions is a key skill that many, especially those embarking on research, must develop. The ability to recognize and to be able to differentiate between scientific and non-scientific questions is also a key component of scientific literacy. If students can understand the characteristics of good scientific questions, that knowledge and understanding can be applied in other areas. Allied to this is the need to develop critical thinking skills and criteria, again something that is applicable to many different areas of the curriculum – from looking at evidence in history to problem solving in technology.

What we must first recognize is that the ability to devise scientific questions which can be tested and the ability to think critically about the evidence and data we present students with will not come naturally and will need careful teaching (see also Chapter 7). A common problem in teaching and learning is making assumptions about what our students can and cannot do. Tasks which we see as basic and intrinsic to lessons, such as group work, discussion, working in pairs etc. often form part of the lesson plan without the necessary step of checking whether or not the students have the skills and ability to carry out the task in the first place. We can all too easily forget to check on whether the class is aware of the different roles that people can undertake in group work, or how we should conduct a discussion and develop arguments in order to 'win' a debate or contribute something meaningful to the lesson. We are perhaps guilty of making these assumptions, then surprised when the class does not perform or behave as expected.

We do not expect our students to come from their primary schools with the practical skills of being able to set up an experiment without some form of instruction or demonstration. In much the same way we should instruct and where possible demonstrate how to formulate scientific questions and how to think critically.

Reflective task

Devise a set of scientific and non-scientific questions that could be posed in the various units of work studied across key stages 3 and 4. Discuss the key elements of scientific questions and ensure that periodically lessons revise and reflect on what makes a scientific question.

Classroom task

Imagine you were testing the characteristics of strawberries and you were working for a food company. You need to find out what people think about your strawberries. To do this you need to set up some tests which you could ask members of the public to do. In small groups create a list of all the possible things you could ask about which may influence people in buying strawberries. Now separate the list into two sections – questions that are scientific and which could be investigated scientifically and questions that are not scientific. Once you have your two groups explain why some questions are scientific and others are not. Are there any common characteristics for the questions which you think are scientific?

References

Bailin, S. 2002. Critical thinking and science education. *Science & Education*, 11, 361–375.

Herrenkohl, L. R., Palincsar, A. S., Dewater, L. S. and Kawasaki, K. 1999. Developing scientific communities in classrooms: a sociocognitive approach. *Journal of the Learning Sciences*, 8, 451–493.

Norris, S. P. 1985. Synthesis of research on critical thinking. *Educational Leadership*, 40–45.

Schwarz, C. V. and White, B. Y. 2005. Metamodeling knowledge: developing students' understanding of scientific modeling. *Cognition and Instruction*, 23, 165–205.

Williams, J. D. 2007a. Do we know How Science Works? A brief history of the scientific method. *School Science Review*, 89, 119–124.

Williams, J. D. 2007b. Just How Does Science Work: the scientific method and key stage 4 science. In: Burton, N., ed. ATSE Annual Conference: Resourcing Initial Teacher Training, 2007b Newport, South Wales. Association for Science Education, 61–80.

Williams, J. D. 2008. Science now and then: discovering how science works. *School Science Review*, 90, 45–46.

6

Is This How Science Works?

The History of science teaches only too plainly the lesson that no single method is absolutely to be relied upon.

(*John William Strutt (1842–1919) – physicist*)

The phrase 'How Science Works' was introduced with the revisions of the national curriculum that took place at key stage 4 in 2006 and key stage 3 in 2008. It heralded the move, outlined in Chapter 1, from teaching 'content' to teaching 'process'. The fear that the science curriculum has been 'dumbed down' is, in reality, unfounded. The content can remain – it is the approach which determines the shift from delivering science as a factual subject where rote learning and reproduction of ideas/diagrams etc. is common, to understanding how scientific knowledge is constructed and developed and how science determines what 'is' and what 'is not' in the natural world. The factual content of old can still be delivered; it just has to be delivered from the perspective of How Science Works (HSW).

How Science Works and the nature of science

The body of knowledge that we call science (which is made up of several disciplines and several interconnecting bodies of knowledge) has been constructed from the observations and experiments, gathered and conducted by countless people over many centuries. Scientists and non-scientists alike try to find patterns in the observations they make since this helps to organize, categorize and make sense of the information gathered. Humans have an affinity for patterns and we can often see patterns where none exist. Students (and adults) will see shapes in clouds from teddy bears to castles. People will filter selectively the information and create rules where none exist, such as having 'intuitive' ideas about buses coming in groups rather than at set times according to published timetables. We see design in nature when there clearly was no 'designer' and our ability to recognize randomness is not well developed either (see Figure 6.1). We are also guilty of using the language of

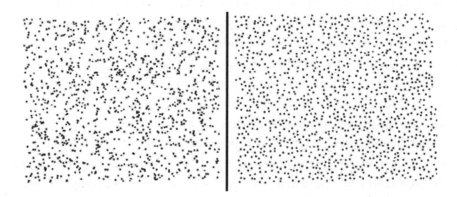

Figure 6.1 Random dots
Most people pick the right hand diagram as randomly generated dots. The left hand diagram is truely randomised showing small clusters of dots

design when describing natural objects – 'the bird's wing is perfectly designed to help it fly' – we see no general problem with a sentence such as this, but in reality the bird's wing has evolved, it was not designed and evolution is no designer, it is a concept or explanation for what we observe in the development and diversity of life. Evolution has no creative mind.

We also attribute human features and characteristics to non-human things. Seeing the Image of the Virgin Mary in toast; the anthropomorphism of animals and inanimate objects; empowering animals with human emotions or human consciousness where they may be none. The domestic cat does not kill birds out of malice – it has no need to kill, normally, as it will be well fed. Yet when the cat brings its offering to the door our instinct is to tell the cat that it has been 'naughty', it shouldn't kill the birds or mice it finds. The cat has no concept of good or bad, it kills through instinct, its offering is probably more an invitation to us to learn how to kill in order that we may feed and be fed.

As a species we make generalizations about underlying fundamental processes. Science is a process that should eliminate intuition, reject design where none exists (e.g. clouds as architectural features) and the job of scientists is to find actual, not supposed, patterns and real generalizations which can be applied to the natural world (universe). In order to do this, scientists must follow some form of methodology or other. The term 'scientific method' is often employed to describe this process, but here we enter a problematic area for the non-scientist, who may conceive of a 'general scientific method', something that we have already discussed as having little to no validity when conceiving of science and How Science Works. How Science Works is intimately linked to the nature of science. The nature of science tells us what is and what is not scientific. Astronomy is scientific, astrology is not. Evolution is scientific, creationism/intelligent design is not. Astrology may lay claim to aspects of a scientific methodology and intelligent design may utilize real science. Ultimately neither astrology nor creationism/intelligent design will pass the test of being scientific. Astrologers may talk about the motion of the stars, the relationships between the planets of our solar system, but its explanations and predictions are unscientific and not testable. Likewise creationism and intelligent design may claim to use the observations and evidence from biology and geology, but its predictions and explanations also are unscientific and not testable. In establishing what is and what is not science we must have an understanding of the nature of science, in establishing How Science Works, we must also have recourse to the nature of science.

Experiments and the scientific method

Scientists will experiment as well as measure and observe the natural world. It is this aspect of science which in part is determined by and determines a scientific method. The methods for experimentation used by the organic chemist are necessarily different from those used by theoretical physicists, which in turn will be different from those used by the geologist or astrophysicists. Each will try to find patterns through experimentation. How and where these scientists operate (one in the chemistry laboratory, another perhaps in the field as well as the laboratory and the theoretical physicist mostly through computer modelling and simulation) means that the methods they use will differ quite considerably. That is not to say that the chemist or geologist cannot use mathematical modelling or computer simulation since they clearly can and do, from modelling molecular structures to earthquakes and volcanic eruptions as well as recreating 3-dimensional models of extinct animals from squashed and flattened fossils.

A key aspect of scientific work, to a greater or lesser extent, is undertaking controlled scientific experiments. The main characteristic of controlled experiments is the ability to control one variable at a time. An outcome of the controlled experiment may be to determine the cause of an effect. Such experiments should also be able to be reproduced. The reproducibility can be a central feature of scientific knowledge in that if an experiment is not able to be reproduced (e.g. in the case of cold fusion – see pages 147–149) then this means that the claims made by scientists are lessened if not rejected wholesale.

In some cases controlled experiments are not possible, as in the field of astronomy. This does not mean that astronomy cannot be regarded as a true science that is capable of claiming scientific truths. The method employed – which is the gathering of data from a variety of sources such as space telescopes and earth-based observatories, probes and satellites – will analyse the energy emissions in the form of electromagnetic radiation and interpret these data to produce explanations of phenomena.

Astronomy also has an interesting facet which few other sciences can claim. Astronomy has an element of time travel in-built. By looking further away from earth we are in effect looking back in time. While some sciences may claim to be able to see a snapshot of past time (e.g. palaeontology and other related earth sciences) astronomy does afford us the opportunity to observe the past as it happens. A simple 'fact' that many students enjoy is the notion that the position of the sun in the sky (when looked at with suitable health and safety in place such as sun-block filters) as observed is actually where the sun was some 8 minutes into the past. Reflected light from the moon takes approximately 1.3 seconds. Looking at these objects could, in effect, be likened to looking at the past. Light coming from far-away objects allows us to see that the laws of physics are general, that is laws of physics described on earth are the same throughout the known universe.

The most distant object observable without a telescope is the Andromeda galaxy which is approximately 2.8×10^{19} kilometres from the earth. Given that the speed of light is about 300,000 kilometres per second, the light from Andromeda has taken almost 3 million years to reach earth. Andromeda is, therefore, 3 million light years away. Telescopes afford us the opportunity to observe many celestial objects much further away. We can observe the evolution of the universe over time. We can see that the same laws of physics apply across its 15-billion-year lifetime.

Scientific models

Most sciences will use models to explain fundamental processes. These models will provide simplified ways of understanding what can be complex processes. The models will have strengths and weaknesses. For example, a common model used to describe the flow of electricity in a circuit utilizes the idea of a water tank (batteries/cells) and pipes through which the water can flow. A weakness in this model is the idea that some students acquire, which is that electricity can, like water, leak if a cable (pipe) is cut or damaged. In scientific terms this could be considered as a weak model. Physicists may also complain that this idea is not in fact a model but an analogy. For a scientific model to be useful it must allow for predictions which are testable. Astronomers make observations; these, in turn, result in hypotheses which can produce predictions which can be tested by making other observations of similar or related phenomena. For astronomers many of these hypotheses are generated and the predictions made having processed the original observations in computer models. In this branch of science, computer modelling and observation have links which, if not present would make astronomy no more than observational and its status of 'science' questionable. Before the advent of computers and computer modelling astronomy still had modelling at its heart from the paper-based calculations and predictions (mathematical models) to the physical models constructed of the movement of planetary bodies in the solar system, the orrery.

Scientific truth

Scientific theories which provide explanations and which can correctly predict new results from new observations or experiments can provide us with a scientific truth. This scientific truth is not the same as a religious 'truth' or a legal definition of truth. It is an accepted explanation of a natural phenomenon. That explanation is held to be 'true' by the majority of the scientific community. It is not a fixed scientific truth which, even in the face of contrary evidence must prevail, but a provisional scientific truth which is necessary for the scientific community to function. All of science is provisional in that new evidence and observations can change our ideas of how and why things happen. For example the continents, once assumed to be fixed, are now not considered fixed. Species were once considered fixed and are now known to be subject to evolutionary processes. Sometimes scientific truth may contradict other 'truths' such as the scientific fact of evolution contradicting the Biblical account of fixed species appearing all at one time. For a small minority this contradiction poses immense problems and requires a reinterpretation of the scientific evidence or, when such reinterpretation is not possible a rejection of such evidence in order for them to uphold what they see as a higher truth – special creation. For the vast majority of scientists, including those who hold religious beliefs, there is no need to reject the science in favour of the unscientific (the Bible or some other Holy book or tract). It is the interpretation of the stories of the Bible or the stories of creation as allegorical which removes the need to reject the science. For some, the simple fact that evolution is about the development and diversity of life on earth and that this theory – which provides a strong, enduring, much tested explanation of the biological and palaeontological evidence – actually does not provide an explanation for the origin of life which allows many scientists to hold two seemingly contradictory views at one time.

How scientists pursue knowledge is the subject of this chapter. What method or methods they utilize, what procedures they adopt and how they make sense of the data (evidence) they collect define how scientists work. The problem, for school science, is that far from there being a simple description for how scientists work, there is no one agreed way of working, no one scientific method and often no agreed simple definitions for the key terminology used by scientists.

A model for How Science Works

Exactly how a scientist works (see Chapter 11) and, therefore How Science Works, depends as much on what knowledge and explanations they are seeking as much as how they conceive of their own scientific discipline. The methods followed by the theoretical physicist to predict the existence of as yet undiscovered sub-atomic particles can be as different from the method followed by organic chemists, intent on discovering the properties and structure of an intracellular protein as the difference between a mathematician and musician investigating the properties of an equation or a symphony.

At the time of writing, there has been little consensus in the science education community on a model for How Science Works. In 2008 I proposed a simple model (Figure 6.2) which would help define aspects of the history,

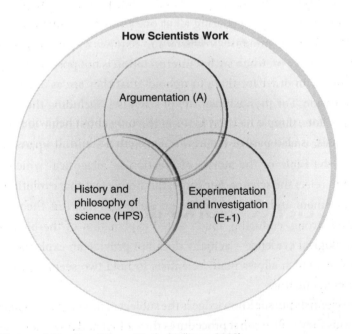

Figure 6.2 A model for How Science Works (Williams, 2008)

philosophy and processes of science such as argumentation, experimentation and investigation, within which teachers and pupils could locate various scientists and their approaches to their day-to-day work (Williams, 2008).

The key to this model is not that it is a fixed idea about how science works, more that it is a guiding framework within which teachers and pupils can locate various science 'workers' or scientists to help guide their understanding of the nature of the job they are completing. For example an organic chemist carrying out laboratory-based work may reside within the E+I spheres, with little to no consideration of the history and philosophy of science. A researcher dealing with embryonic stem cell research resides within spheres A and E+I as their work must consider moral and ethical dimensions. A theoretical physicist may reside within the HPS and E+I spheres.

The model allows us to consider how scientists approach their work and situates different sciences within different spheres. The model is also useful in that it can accommodate those who see themselves as 'scientists', but who others may not consider as traditional scientists in the standard models of biology, chemistry, physics, geology and astronomy. Psychology, for example is that branch of science which deals with the study of brain function and behaviour in humans and other animals. Psychologists may study things such as how we think, how we perceive things. They study emotions, motivation behaviour, our intra- and interpersonal relationships. To do this they use a scientific method, they gather data, they determine causal relationships or they look for correlations between relationships. Psychologists will employ empirical methods, they use deduction and induction, test hypotheses and develop theories. A psychologist would easily fit into some of the spheres in Figure 6.2, for example E+I. Psychology, learning about behaviour in humans and animals, is also part of the new science curriculum. It forms part of the suite of specifications that encompass science.

How Science Works and the National Strategy

The original vision for How Science Works when it was introduced by the Qualifications and Curriculum Authority (QCA)[1] was very limited. It included the rather vague notion that it involved the 'scientific method'. With the revision of the curriculum at key stage 3 and key stage 4, How Science

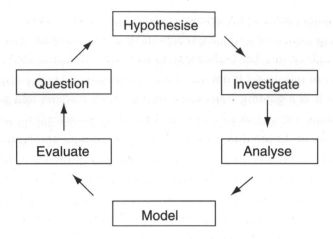

Figure 6.3 The ThinkerTools scientific inquiry cycle. This inquiry cycle is slightly modified from the one used in the prior ThinerTools Inquiry Curriculum (see White & Frederiksen, 1998)

Works became a formal part of the science curriculum. Work by the National Strategies combined the ideas outlined in the QCA vision and the curriculum reforms to produce a more coherent vision of How Science Works.

There is a temptation to think of How Science Works as merely an approach to what was previously called Scientific Enquiry. From the inception of the national curriculum document until the recent revisions, Scientific Enquiry (that part of the national curriculum often labelled Sc1) encompassed the experimental and investigative part of science. Figure 6.3 shows a generalized model for Scientific Enquiry. It was skills based and looked at the process of carrying out experiments and problem solving. It looked at the planning of experiments and investigations, obtaining, analysing and evaluating evidence. This standard approach to the practical side of science is enduring and is still likely to have strong supporters. For the National Strategies, *How Science Works* is more than just scientific enquiry. It is intended to encourage pupils to develop as critical and creative thinkers and who are also problem solvers. The National Strategy approach to How Science Works promotes two areas of skills development:

- Explanations, argument and decisions
- Practical and enquiry skills.

Developing explanations of natural phenomena is the driving force of the discipline of science. Any approach, such as How Science Works, which claims to be the process of science must have at its heart this explanatory paradigm. Aligned with this is the ability to explore ideas, test ideas and produce evidence for and against ideas. The practical side of science – its experiments and investigations – is also then a key skill that we must develop in our pupils. Effective enquiry work would involve exploring questions and finding answers '*through the gathering and evaluation of evidence. Pupils need to understand how evidence comes from the collection and critical interpretation of both primary and secondary data and how evidence may be influenced by contexts such as culture, politics or ethics* (National Strategies, n.d).

Explanations, argument and decisions

This aspect of How Science Works is different from the practical approach to scientific investigations, but as noted above is essential to the process. It encompasses

- Developing explanations using ideas and models (Chapter 5)
- Challenge and collaboration in the development of explanation (Chapter 2)
- Developing argument (Chapter 7)
- Application, implications and cultural understanding (Chapter 8)
- Communication for audience and with purpose (Chapter 10).

Aspects of these strands have been further developed in this book under different chapter headings as noted.

Practical and enquiry skills

While the old 'Sc1' approach is persistent, it has been modified for HSW to the idea of using investigative approaches in the following areas:

- Planning an approach
- Selecting and managing variables
- Assessing risk and working safely
- Obtaining and presenting primary evidence
- Working critically with primary evidence
- Working critically with secondary evidence.

The main change in approach is a greater focus on the critical interpretation and evaluation of secondary evidence, as well as providing reliable evidence for the development of explanations. This latter change links the two main strands of How Science Works.

How Science Works: The National Strategy journey

The National Strategy envisages the acquisition of the key components of HSW as a journey with 4 key elements: The *How Science Works* journey can be thought of as having four key elements.

- The development of a range of practical enquiry skills to enable pupils to gather reliable and valid evidence which includes the planning of an enquiry, the gathering of data and other evidence and the drawing of conclusions.
- The ability to process and evaluate evidence from secondary sources.
- The ability to use evidence to produce and test explanations.
- The ability to present and share explanations to a variety of audiences and to understand how the scientific communities function to strengthen the quality of explanations.

The shift for science teachers and science teaching must be away from the idea that the practical and investigative aspect of science can be delivered independently from other aspects of science.

> How science works should be an integral part of science teaching and not a 'bolt-on" or mechanical, recipe-following activity. Teachers need to be clear about whether a practical activity is being used in an illustrative way, i.e. to develop scientific knowledge and understanding, or to provide a context to develop an aspect of How Science Works.
>
> (National Strategies, n.d)

How Science Works in the specifications

The delivery of How Science Works in the GCSE specifications (for examination up to 2010) will vary slightly from board to board. In general there tends to be a bias towards the experimental/investigative nature of HSW rather than other aspects.

The assessment objectives (AO) related to HSW are common to all GCSE specifications:

- demonstrate knowledge and understanding of the scientific facts, concepts, techniques and terminology in the specification;
- show understanding of how scientific evidence is collected and its relationship with scientific explanations and theories;
- show understanding of how scientific knowledge and ideas change over time and how these changes are validated.

The AQA specification provides a rationale as well as a glossary of terms to complement the introduction of HSW. In its rationale, it acknowledges that science as a discipline is an attempt to explain the world in which we live. It goes on to talk about the way in which technology can have an impact on society and the environment.

The key aspect of their interpretation is how science and scientists use evidence. In particular how that evidence should be both reliable and valid in order to support appropriate conclusions. If a prime consideration of the need to teach science is to develop a scientifically literate population then knowing about the reliability and validity of evidence is key to this aim (see Chapter 9). AQA usefully set out some key characteristics that scientists and the scientifically literate need to consider, these are:

- how we observe the world
- designing investigations so that patterns and relationships between variables may be identified
- making measurements by selecting and using instruments effectively
- presenting and representing data
- identifying patterns, relationships and making suitable conclusions.

How Science Works and twenty-first-century science

A driving force for the introduction of How Science Works into the national curriculum for science is the development of twenty-first-century science. This approach to science and the GCSE specifications developed arose from work conducted in the late 1990s. The report of this important review of science education, *Beyond 2000* (Millar and Osborne, 1998), sought to define what science education should look like beyond the millennium. On the issue of How Science Works (though this term was not in use during the research and reporting of the review of science education) the report noted that

> We also believe that young people need an understanding of how scientific inquiry is conducted – to help them appreciate the reasoning which underpins scientific knowledge claims, so that they are better able to appreciate both the strengths and the limitations of such claims, in a range of situations and contexts.
>
> We would, however, suggest that the argument that an understanding of the methods of scientific inquiry is practically useful in everyday contexts has been over-emphasised. For most purposes a systematic, common-sense approach will suffice.
>
> (Millar and Osborne, 1998, pp. 11–12)

In the subsequently developed specification this was developed into 'ideas about science'. People, it was argued, needed more than just an understanding of the concepts and ideas of science. They saw pupils and people in general as consumers of scientific knowledge who needed more than just knowledge and understanding about the ideas. People needed to be able to reflect a wide range of things if they were truly going to be considered as 'scientifically literate'. These included:

- the practices that have produced scientific knowledge;
- the kinds of reasoning that are used in developing a scientific argument and
- the issues that arise when scientific knowledge is put to practical use.

Conclusion

Although we are gaining a more consistent view of How Science Works, it is clear that, just as there is no single 'scientific method' so too is there no single approach, model or definition of How Science Works. Different specifications and different writers have varying views of what HSW means in practice.

The terminology used in conjunction with HSW is also varied and not consistent across the textbooks, specifications and supporting material for HSW (see Chapter 9 for a set of definitions of key terminology). Teachers must, therefore develop their own individual understanding of How Science Works through an examination of the component parts where these component parts do have consistency. It is clear that How Science Works is not just teaching practical techniques and investigations and 'doing' experiments. It is also clear that new ways of working and new approaches to science teaching are now required. Critical thinking has a higher profile than before, as does history and philosophy of science. Argumentation – which has been recognized as a fundamental characteristic of a good science education – which involves teaching pupils the skills required to follow scientific arguments and debates in the public domain is also now, more than ever, important if we are to achieve a scientifically literate society.

What was an 'add-on' to science lessons, for example looking at moral and ethical stances and considering the impact of new technologies, or simply being able to critically evaluate the evidence for and against in arguments over mobile 'phone masts, cloning and the use of chemical pesticides over organic farming methods is now more integral to the teaching of science. What is clear is that this cannot be done without an understanding of the science behind each of these issues and so the delivery of content is not reduced, just refocused. The age old 'why do I need to know this' from bored pupils may well be lessened as they see the relevance and context of the science in the form of How Science Works and its importance to their everyday lives.

That which was once referred to as Sc1 is still part of How Science Works but, as the beyond 2000 report hinted, it should not be the overwhelming and overriding approach. The change from teaching a fact-based approach to science to a process-based approach is a way of delivering scientific literacy for the majority of our pupils. The approach must still, however, deliver enough content to allow those who seek to go further in their scientific studies to As, A level and beyond. A key misunderstanding of the new science curriculum is the apparent lack of 'content'. This leads to an incorrect conclusion that the curriculum has been 'dumbed down' and that much of the useful scientific facts and content is no longer to be delivered.

Reflective task

Consider Figure 6.2. Is this a good model for How Science Works? Could the model be expanded upon or changed to be more in line with the concept of HSW? What sort of a model would you construct for HSW?

Note

1. The QCA was renamed the Qualifications, Curriculum and Development Agency (QCDA). In May 2010 the QCDA was earmarked for closure by the new coalition government which took office on 12 May.

References

Millar, R. and Osborne, J. 1998. Beyond 2000: science education for the future, London: King's College.

National Strategies, D. n.d. *How Science Works* [Online]. London: DCSF. [Accessed 20January 2010].

Williams, J. D. 2008. Science now and then: discovering how science works. *School Science Review,* 90, 45–46.

Argumentation in Science

7

All silencing of discussion is an assumption of infallibility.

(John Stuart Mill (1806–1873) philosopher)

Do scientists argue? Of course they do. The arguments are rarely, if ever, violent, but the history of science is littered with arguments. The argument between Isaac Newton (1642–1727) and Gottfried Liebniz (1646–1716) over who first discovered and described calculus is a famous case in point. Newton claimed to have begun working on a form of the calculus in 1666, but did not publish anything until decades later and Liebniz, who began working on his version of calculus in 1674, published in 1684. There are many other instances of such 'priority arguments' in the history of science. Is this the same, however, as the process of argumentation?

Science is founded on argumentation, rather than argument. Knowledge in science will not be accepted unless and until the process of argumentation establishes the authority of that knowledge. This process of argumentation, as opposed to argument, is not just about priority – who did what, when and, therefore, who should be proclaimed the true originator of an idea or the prime discoverer of a concept, process or object. The process of argumentation is much more complex and is, it could be claimed, fundamental to the process and progress of science. You could also contend that learning requires argumentation. Language is core to learning and the discourse of science – the language interaction – that takes place in the science classroom is a key component of learning. This language use in the classroom is often referred to as a spoken discourse.

In this chapter we will look at how we talk about science in the classroom, what the nature of science classroom discourse is, as well as considering how scientists construct arguments. We will consider what we mean by argumentation and how argumentation can be an effective tool in learning and understanding scientific principles and concepts.

Talking science

If you sit and observe science teachers going about their normal daily work, it will not be long before you think about the language they use. In science teacher education, the nature of scientific language, the specialist terms we use and the 'correctness' of the use of language in science is a core part of understanding the process of teaching and learning science. From simple things such as the correct use of data or datum – the plural and singular – to teaching students how to correctly describe processes, teachers play an important role in guiding talk in science lessons. Even guiding students on the specific and general use of identical terms plays its part in science teaching, for example that the word cell has multiple meanings dependent on the context within which it is used (biology, physics, law and order, etc.). The idea that every science lesson is also a language lesson (Wellington and Osborne, 2001), where not only do we have to consider what science is being taught, but how that science is taught and how the language of science has a particular structure based on Greek and Latin, is fundamental to planning for effective learning. Teachers routinely point out the etymology, or origin, of scientific words. They will break them down into component parts to show how the word relates to the concept, for example, *photosynthesis* or 'making (synthesis)' with 'light (photo)'. They may even relate the word to other common uses of the same stems – *photograph* (drawing with light). When teachers are asked about literacy in science (as opposed to scientific literacy) and how literacy is addressed in science lessons, it is such descriptions that are uppermost. If we ask about 'talking' about science in the science classroom, or science classroom discourse, we will not necessarily get a response that is about the process of argumentation in science.

Studies of teachers' science classroom discourses show that a common pattern is that of Initiation, Response, Feedback (IRF).[1] A teacher asks a question, a pupil responds and the teacher provides feedback on that response. Throughout this type of conversation the teacher retains control and guides the direction of the conversation. A major limitation of such a classroom discourse is that on the whole teachers will only initiate questions on things for which they already know the answer. Such questions have been referred to as 'pseudo-questions' (Kelly, 2007) as their purpose is about ascertaining if the pupils know what the teacher knows. The questions are not about what the pupil *thinks* or *understands* about the concepts or processes under discussion. Lemke called this type of classroom discussion a 'triadic dialogue'. He put forward the idea that the learning of science was intimately linked to how we talk about science. '*students have to learn to combine the meanings of different terms according to accepted ways of talking science*' (1990).

There is a distinction to be made between talking science and talking about science. Talking about science involves observing, describing, comparing, classifying, discussing, questioning, challenging, generalizing and reporting. In many science classrooms a number of these take place on a daily basis, but some aspects of talking science are not emphasized enough, for example discussing, challenging and reporting. Actually 'talking science' rather than simply regurgitating known science (which is more talking about science) is limited in many classrooms. Talking is a social activity but talking science in science classrooms is not routinely a social activity. For it to become a routine social activity it has to be planned and enacted. It will not happen naturally. It also requires a change in the thinking of the teacher. A move away from a transmission model of teaching where the teacher controls the science content, its delivery (the transmission of facts that should be recorded and memorized) and what is done with that content (the regurgitation of the factual content within a testing or examination framework). Talking science and using the language of science in the form of argumentation is not necessarily about the factual content of science. In the transmission model of science teaching (and learning) where content is the crucial 'thing' to be delivered, discussion, comparison even analysis and synthesis are less important than knowledge.

Knowledge of science is different from understanding of science and scientific literacy – a prime goal of science education. This is neatly illustrated by Dennis Skinner MP who, in a debate on selectivity and Grammar schools in 1996 said,

> I went to (a Grammar school) and they taught me Latin – amo, amas, amat, amamus, amatis, amant. They also taught me the Archimedes principle – when a body is weighed in air and then in a fluid, the upthrust or apparent loss in weight is equal to the weight of the fluid displaced. But none of that equipped me for life. I went down a coal mine, which is where I got my real education.

Apparently Dennis Skinner didn't think that mere knowledge of 'Archimedes' principle' was 'an education'. Rote learning facts in science or being able to recite a 'principle' many years after the event is, indeed, not an education. It would be the application of the principle that would determine if an education in Archimedes' principle had been achieved. Even setting an examination question would not necessarily determine if knowledge of Archimedes' principle had been translated into understanding of that principle. With rote learning comes an ability to reproduce what appear to be high-quality answers to questions, but with no other attributes such as understanding or application. In the science classroom, asking questions that require a simple recitation of the principle also does not test understanding. Such low-level questioning (see Bloom's cognitive domain figure 8.2 p. 106) can leave teachers with a false impression of the degree of scientific understanding that pupils have.

As stated, language is core to learning. One view of learning is that it is the product of the difference between the intuitive models that we hold and the newer ideas or models that we come across. Learning and understanding is the journey between the old model and the new model (Osborne, 2010: 328). That journey is characterized by the arguments (internal or external) that the learner has. If the learner has an old, intuitive model by which they understand a scientific idea or concept, but the 'science lesson' presents new models or ideas which may contradict that intuitive model, to undertake the journey from old to new knowledge – to learn the new idea – a series of 'arguments' has to take place. Those arguments may be internal and based within the consciousness of the learner or they may be external and involve arguments with peers and/or teachers.

Arguing (in the sense of 'argumentation' rather than in the sense of having a disagreement) a case is not something that is intuitive and natural to students. The art and skill of argumentation needs to be taught and understood by the learner. The skills the learner needs can be acquired through the delivery of what is commonly called 'thinking skills'. There is research evidence that shows that the development of thinking skills can be achieved through specific interventionist approaches. For science education, one of the most widely known of these approaches is CASE (Cognitive Acceleration through Science Education). This was a project, again developed at King's College London, that took 30 specific lessons designed to teach reasoning across the first 2 years of secondary education. Those reasoning skills were developed around a Piagetian model of child development and were designed to accelerate the students through Piaget's defined levels (see Table 7.1). Mounting evidence shows that the CASE intervention does improve students' learning (Shayer and Adey, 1993). Developing good argumentation skills is about learning to think. It is also about the construction of new understandings about 'old' models and ideas. The effect of the CASE intervention was not restricted to science. Gains in pupil achievement were also found in mathematics, languages and arts-based subjects.

Scientists have ways of reaching conclusions about the ideas and experiments they consider and undertake. Providing students with an understanding of how scientists either inductively or deductively come to conclusions is useful in setting the scene for their subsequent consideration of scientific data and viewpoints.

Scientific arguments

The two dominant 'methods' or ways of reaching conclusions in science are deductivism and inductivism. Both methods use reasoning as their modus

Table 7.1 Piaget's stages in child development

Stage	Characteristics
Sensori-motor (Birth–2 yrs)	Is able ability to differentiate 'self' from other objects
	Is able to recognize 'self' as the agent of an action
	Begins to demonstrate intentional acts for example hit a button on a toy to produce music
	Realizes that things continue to exist even if undetected by the senses (e.g. even if they are unable to see or feel an object)
Pre-operational (2–7 years)	Uses language and to represent objects by images and words
	Has difficulty seeing things from the viewpoint of others
	Is able to classify objects but usually only by a single characteristic for example colour, shape, size etc.
Concrete operational (7–11 years)	Is able to think logically about objects and events
	Is able to understand the principle of conservation of:
	number (age 6)
	mass (age 7)
	weight (age 9)
	Classifies objects according to several features and can order them in series along a single dimension such as size.
Formal operational (11 years and up)	Can think logically about abstract propositions and test hypotheses systematically
	Becomes concerned with the hypothetical, the future and ideological problems

This forms the basis of the CASE interventionist approach to developing logical/thinking skills. There is evidence to suggest that this strict linking of stages to absolute ages is too rigid. Many students will be able to manage concrete operations earlier than Piaget thought. Some people may never reach the formal operational stage or are not presented with opportunities to develop this stage in everyday life. Piaget's approach is known as 'cognitive constructivism'. Others put greater emphasis on the part played by language and interactions with other people in enabling students to learn.

operandi, both have strengths and weaknesses in their operation. What is unclear from the examination specifications and the approach to How Science Works currently being taken is whether the distinction between these two approaches has been made clear to teachers and pupils alike.

The structure of reasoning and argumentation within science is important and constitutes part of the 'method' followed by all scientists. Arguments begin with a proposition: The earth is round; my cat has four legs; rain is composed of water; raspberries are red. Propositions can be true or false. Not all propositions however can be easily divided into true or false, for example the proposition 'bacterial life once existed on Mars' may be true or false. The main point of a logical or reasoned argument is how one proposition may be connected to another and the 'truth' of those propositions. When constructing a logical argument the idea is for the propositions (the premises) to support the conclusion. The step between the premise(s) and the conclusion is the inference.

A simple argument with a set of true premises and a valid conclusion could be: My cousin Richard is a medical doctor; all medical doctors attend medical school therefore Richard went to medical school. A true premise does not always guarantee a valid outcome even if the logic or argument is itself correct, for example a bat has wings, all birds have wings therefore a bat is a bird. Both of the premises are true, but the conclusion is invalid. This is of course due to the way that science has decided which features are the ones that distinguish how we classify organisms. This serves to show some of the issues presented when reasoning in science from a deductive position only.

Deductive reasoning is most commonly found in the discipline of mathematics. Proofs of theorems have been the nightmare of many students over the years – less so in today's approach to mathematics, but utilizing a deductive approach in mathematics allows for proof and with it, truth and certainty. While some scientists undoubtedly use deductive reasoning to arrive at answers to their problems, equating such scientific reasoning with absolute proof and truth in science cannot happen. No matter the degree of confirmation for a scientific explanation, it can only be held as provisional as it is always possible for a scientific fact to be shown to be wrong or incorrect for example as in the case above of plate tectonics revolutionizing our understanding of the movement of continents over the earth's surface.

As noted previously (Chapter 2), much of science until the time of Francis Bacon was deductive in its reasoning. A strong deductive conclusion can be made when the information or data that supports such a conclusion is, itself valid. With deductive reasoning in science, rather than talk of proof we talk about conclusions being valid or invalid. It is possible, as we have already seen, to come to an invalid conclusion.

Inductive reasoning proceeds in a different way. The outcome of inductive reasoning does not necessarily lead to a valid or invalid conclusion. It is more a case of the probability of the conclusion being more or less valid. The strength of inductive reasoning is in the number of initial supporting instances for the conclusion. For example, driving to Wales I observe 200 sheep in a field. All the sheep are white therefore I may infer that in the next farm I drive past which contains a flock of sheep, all are likely to be white. While the first premise may be true and while I may have 200 data items, my conclusion cannot be said to be valid or true. The 200 sheep, which in data terms is a lot of data points or observations, is a very small sample of the total possible numbers of sheep alive today. I may say that it is likely or more probable that the sheep will be white, but I cannot rule out observing a black sheep. Inductive reasoning involves moving from a specific set of facts (data) to a general conclusion. The more representative your data are of the total possible data, the more valid will be the outcome.

Whether a scientist uses deductive and/or inductive reasoning will depend on whether or not the work that they are doing is theory building or theory confirming. With deductive reasoning, a general principle or established theory in science is the initial premise from which a valid conclusion can be inferred. Where scientists are seeking to develop explanations from their observations or data then induction is the method followed. For science and the scientific method then, it is not a case of either/or deduction/induction. Science can, and does, utilize both approaches to establish the validity of an argument or to test the established, prevailing explanations.

Argumentation in the science classroom

Argumentation, it has been advocated, is a core practice of science and, as such, an essential aspect of science education. Talk in science classrooms (and other classrooms) tends to be dominated by teacher talk rather than student talk. There is often discussion about the 'mistake stigma' which prevents pupil talk for fear of making a mistake. The object of education is to not make mistakes, which are seen as 'bad', but to be correct, which is seen as 'good'. The mistake stigma then relates to students being viewed as 'bad' rather than 'good' if the answer to any teacher initiated question is incorrect (McNeill and Pimentel, 2009).

The move from fact-based teaching of science to process teaching within the framework of How Science Works views science not as a body of facts that should (must) be learned, but as a product of social discourse and refinement of ideas and concepts, with some concepts being changed over time so that they bear only a passing resemblance to the initially generated idea. Many scientific ideas and concepts have been discarded over time as evidence contradicts initial thoughts and ideas. Science appears to move away from being a socially generated 'of its time' discipline to one where there are inherent 'truths' and established facts and ideas. Earlier in this book (see Chapter 1) we looked at the nature of science and how all ideas in science are provisional – even those that are well established. Contradictory evidence can overturn an established scientific 'truth'. Some argue that science seeks to do this all the time. The testing of ideas, the seeking of falsification for an idea is seen by some scientists as the test of whether an idea is scientific or not.

If we are to achieve scientific literacy for all then our approach to science and science education surely must be consistent. We cannot teach science as an absolute body of facts and knowledge, while 'real' science proceeds through discourse and argument. The currency of science may well be data: observations, measurements etc., but the economy or system of science is how the currency is exchanged between the populations of scientists and how that currency is understood and manipulated by the general public.

> In science classrooms it is important not only for students to be able to make sense of data and construct claims, but they also need to be able to consider alternative claims as well as critique the claims and justifications provided by other individuals in the context of dialogic interactions.
>
> (McNeill and Pimentel, 2009: 206)

The structure of argumentation in the science classroom

The IDEAS project from King's College London was designed to enhance the argumentation skills of secondary science students (Osborne et al., 2004). The materials consist of an in-service workshop pack, which is supported by a DVD of 28 instances of teachers engaging in the kind of teaching necessary to develop students' thinking and reasoning in science. In addition, there is a resources pack to support such teaching approaches in the classroom.

Table 7.2 The language of Argumentation (adapted from the IDEAS Project, King's College, London)

Claims	They are assertions about what exists or values that people hold
Data	The evidence used to support the claim
Warrants	Statements that explain the relationship of the data to the claim
Rebuttals	Statements which contradict the data or warrant
Counter-claims	Opposing assertions

The IDEAS approach was based on the work of Toulmin (1958). Using argumentation in the classroom we do not presume the claims we make to be true – even if, scientifically, we may accept that they are. The process of argumentation is a way of trying to establish the 'truth' of any claim that is made. All claims must be supported by data, and what Toulmin calls 'warrants' which are justifications of the relationship between the claim and the data (see Table 7.2 for definitions of the various terms used). These warrants have backings (the premise or foundation on which the warrant is made) and qualifiers, which establish the limits of any claims under discussion. The process will also contain rebuttals and counter-arguments.

Argumentation can lead to a greater understanding of the science. Students will need to be taught how to argue in science lessons and the teacher will need to rethink the structure of the lesson and, more importantly, the questioning that they undertake in such lessons. There must be a move from simple knowledge-based questions, such as 'what is the name of. . .?' to questions such as 'how do you know?' 'what evidence do you have to support that?' or 'can you think of an argument against your view?'

A science lesson can provide opportunities for groups to engage with science content and develop arguments that support or refute various claims. The development or argument cannot be done without the input of content. In order to defend a claim a student must have data and these data will be linked to science knowledge. Teaching argumentation does not involve abandoning science content. While students can undoubtedly acquire and develop reasoning skills earlier than Piaget's stages suggest, their capability will necessarily be limited by a lack of knowledge content (Osborne, 2010: 465).

With the development of thinking skills (or reasoning skills, or argumentation skills) a prime aim must be the development of certain abilities in our students. Research summarized by Osborne (2010) suggests that the skills that we should seek to develop in science education are an ability

- to identify patterns in data and make inferences
- to coordinate evidence with theory and discriminate between supportive evidence and evidence that is either not supportive or indeterminate
- to construct evidence-based hypotheses or models of scientific phenomena and provide persuasive arguments that justify their validity
- to resolve uncertainty, which requires an understanding of statistical techniques, error and appropriate experimental design

Using argumentation with pure science that is abstract and context free may not necessarily lead to improvements. When context is used and, especially where the framework of the discussion is linked to a social context, this relates to the everyday experiences of the students and, as a result, science lessons are more effective. The use of open questions by the teacher also improves the conversations of the pupils and enhances the development of argumentation skills and science knowledge and understanding (Dawson and Venville, 2008).

Does argumentation improve science learning and understanding?

Fact-based teaching and examinations and tests that assess knowledge over understanding can be misleading. Knowing is not the same as understanding and many students are able to 'know' the answer to a question without necessarily being able to 'understand' the concept or idea on which the question is based. I 'know' that one idea about why things have 'mass' is a consequence of the interactions between the fields surrounding the postulated, but as yet undetected, Higgs boson. Do I understand this? Do I really understand quantum physics? The answer is 'no'. That knowledge, however, brings me in contact – should I so wish – to other pieces of knowledge on quantum physics and my journey to understanding will lie in either internal argumentation which rationalizes and builds on my basic knowledge or, should I be lucky, an opportunity to enter into a form of argumentation and discourse with someone who is more knowledgeable and understanding of quantum physics.

A shift from teaching facts to constructing lessons that are more focused on the processes of science (true How Science Works lessons) requires an element of non-religious faith and belief that such an approach will ultimately deliver better learning in science. Osborne (2010) recounts the results of a meta-analysis of fourteen classes that had been taught using traditional methods, which showed an average 25 per cent gain between pre- and post-test results. By contrast in classes where non-traditional methods were employed (the teacher asked students to discuss concepts and present their findings to the class) there was an average gain of 48 per cent. This, on its own, is not enough to throw all 'traditional teaching' out of the science lab window, but it does indicate that the quality of talking that takes place in the science classroom needs to be recognized and planned for. Discussion, argumentation, rationalization, synthesis and analysis and pupils working in groups to discuss and present, need more attention in our training and continuing professional development of science teachers. The difficulty comes when we recognize that traditional models of teaching and learning where the transmission of ideas, facts and concepts is given priority over teaching the skills of argumentation. This is often for the purpose of 'improving' science examination results, but this purpose may be called into question. Skills in argumentation are not assessed by traditional examination; the examination, to the detriment of the discipline, drives the focus of teaching.

Conclusion

Science proceeds through argumentation of one sort or another – from the laboratory scientist discussing the results of the latest batch of experimental and empirical data, to the moderated argumentation that happens in the peer review process for publication in the scientific journals (see Chapter 10). The process of argumentation is fundamental to the development of the discipline of science. Teaching students the skills of argumentation is teaching them to think and teaching them to understand. The evidence suggests that argumentation will improve understanding and will be evidenced in better examination and test results. The evidence also shows that this improvement will not happen through the teaching of argumentation skills alone. That is, the teaching cannot be content free. There must be content teaching of the science since this is the substance that is used in the argument. Argument without substance will not be effective and will not improve students' scientific literacy.

There is no doubt that teaching science from a process perspective, using How Science Works as a framework, will be a challenge to many teachers who have themselves not been brought through such a science education. There are some inherent dangers in our education system at present, such as the obsession with results over learning. Improved examination results do not, in my view, automatically indicate better understanding. Improved examination results may not even indicate better learning. They merely indicate that the student has got better at doing the examination. If the approach to teaching and learning is focused on examination results rather than thinking and understanding which leads to learning, then we may have year-on-year improvements in examination results, but we will also have year-on-year problems, by producing generations of young people who are unable to grapple with living in an increasingly complex and technologically advanced society. The teaching of argumentation, along with the acquisition of a core of scientific knowledge is therefore central to achieving scientific literacy for all.

Reflective task

Argumentation and discourse in science lessons is of key importance to developing scientific literacy. The quality of argumentation is often an issue in science classes and arguably, it is one of the most important things we can teach students. As a team, reflect on the quality or argumentation in your science lessons and review what skills-based teaching is conducted in science and then in other subjects on 'what makes a good argument' and how to argue successfully. Discuss with colleagues in other subject areas where appropriate skills can be developed and where argumentation can impact on their lessons as well as your science lessons (e.g. geography, history, RE, English etc.).

Classroom task

Being able to argue your case is an important skill. The key to winning an argument is to know the other side of the argument as well as your own. In addition you need to ensure that your argument is logical and sensible.

Choose an issue in science where there are opposing arguments (e.g. for or against cloning, GM foods, the position of mobile phone masts). Decide which 'side' of the argument you agree most with.

To develop a good argument you must

1. make a claim about the issue you are arguing for or against
2. support your claim with some evidence (data)
3. say how your evidence supports your claim
4. think of some counterclaims (rebuttals) which contradict your claim.

Your task now is to create a case for arguing in favour of the counter-claim.

Note

1. This pattern is also sometimes referred to as Initiation, Response and Evaluation (IRE).

References

Dawson, V. and Venville, G. 2008. Teaching strategies for developing students' argumentation skills about socioscientific issues in high school genetics. *Research in Science Education,* 40, 133–148.

Kelly, G. J. 2007. Discourse in Science Classrooms. In: Abell, S. K., Lederman, Norman G. (ed.) *Handbook of Research on Science Education (Paperback)– Routledge,* London: Routledge.

Lemke, J. L. 1990. *Talking Science: Language, Learning, and Values (Language and Classroom Processes, Vol 1),* London: Ablex Publishing.

Mcneill, K. L. and Pimentel, D. S. 2009. Scientific discourse in three urban classrooms: the role of the teacher in engaging high school students in argumentation. *Science Education,* 94, 203–229.

Osborne, J. 2010. Arguing to learn in science: the role of collaborative, critical discourse. *Science,* 328, 463–466.

Osborne, J., Erduran, S. and Simon, S. 2004. Enhancing the quality of argumentation in school science. *Journal of Research in Science Teaching,* 41, 994–1020.

Shayer, M. and Adey, P. S. 1993. Accelerating the development of formal thinking in middle and high school students IV: three years after a two-year intervention. *Journal of Research in Science Teaching,* 30, 351–366.

Toulmin, S. E. 1958. *The Uses of Argument,* Cambridge: Cambridge University Press.
Wellington, J. and Osborne, J. 2001. *Language and Literacy in Science Education,* Buckingham: Open University Press.

Further reading

Erduran, S. and Jimenez-Aleixandre, M. P. (eds) (2008) *Argumentation in Science Education,* New York: Springer.

8 Moral and Ethical Issues in Science Education

It is essential to recognise that reliable scientific knowledge is value-free and has no moral or ethical value. Science tells us how the world is.

(Wolpert, 2004)

Lewis Wolpert makes a distinction between science and technology. Technology, he argues, is the application of scientific knowledge to solving problems. Science, simply, is knowledge. It is only when science is applied, he continues, that moral and ethical considerations come into play. In essence he feels that scientists should be free to discover whatever they can about the natural world and, those discoveries should not be constrained by thoughts about ethics. It is not the scientist who applies his or her knowledge – it is the technologist. Pure science simply describes how the world is (Wolpert, 2004, 2005). For many years the approach to teaching science in schools was just such an approach – the facts of science were taught, morals and ethics did not figure as part of the day-to-day teaching of science; it was, for the most part, a Gradgindian approach to teaching science.

Now, what I want is Facts. Teach these boys and girls nothing but Facts. Facts alone are wanted in life. Plant nothing else, and root out everything else. You can only form the minds of reasoning animals upon Facts: nothing else will ever be of any service to them. This is the principle on which I bring up my own students, and this is the principle on which I bring up these students. Stick to Facts, sir!

(Dickens, 2008: 1)

Moral and ethical considerations only formed part of the teaching approach as an 'extra' dimension of a science lesson, something that added interest and/or context to the science being taught. In this chapter we will look at the moral and ethical dimension of science education and how that is now a more central part of the everyday science lesson.

What do we mean by morals and ethics?

Before we begin to address how morals and ethics constitute a part of the process of science known as How Science Works we need to define what we mean by morals and ethics.

Morals involve the relationship between right and wrong. It is about how individuals or groups behave. A moral stance may be taken by an individual regardless of the rule of law – he or she may choose to act in what they perceive to be a moral way, even if, or sometimes because, the law or rule suggests that they should not act in a particular way. Groups may also have a common standard of justice that may apply. This could be what the group considers to be the 'right' approach. This may, or may not, be in accordance with any official ruling. A person with morals is able to tell right from wrong. An immoral person may know right from wrong but chooses the 'wrong' stance. An amoral person is one who is seemingly without any morals. The issue of right and wrong is very complex. One person's 'right' may be another person's 'wrong'. People may have inner convictions that provide a so-called moral compass. If an issue under discussion is a contentious one, for example the rights of gay people to have a civil partnership, someone who has a strong affiliation to a particular religion may object to what the law allows and insist that the gay couple and the law are wrong, and, as such, are not entitled to be considered alongside conventionally married couples. More particular for science, issues surrounding abortion and contraception may be part of the curriculum and some teachers may have a moral stance on these issues that is at odds with what the law states and permits.

On the other hand, the world's population is made up of many cultures – their norms when it comes to matters with a moral dimension will also vary, for example in some countries it is permissible to drink alcohol, in others it is forbidden. In some cultures it is permissible for women to go topless on a beach, in others women must cover up in public places. The majority of discussions in science education will not involve many religious or culturally moral considerations – though a number of topics in biology may well have this as a core dimension, for example evolution and creationism; cloning and, as indicated above, abortion and birth control etc.

Ethics is about the approach taken by an individual or group of individuals – how their conduct is affected by their moral stance even. Ethical standards are very closely, if not inextricably, linked to moral principles. It is possible for the ethical approach adopted by a scientist to be at odds with their moral standards – where these moral standards are personal. If this were to be the case in all likelihood the scientist would not do the research or would feel compelled to abstain from that part of the research with which they did not agree. Occasionally the scientist may decide to break the ethical code, adjudging that the moral considerations outweighed the accepted ethical approach in a particular instance. For the purposes of school-based science education such moral and ethical dilemmas make for an interesting and contextualized study of scientific ideas, processes and discoveries. The question we need to consider is whether or not this is enough of a justification for teaching science from a moral and ethical standpoint.

Why teach from a moral and ethical standpoint?

If we took the discipline of science, the definition of science made earlier in the book, then there would be a case to argue that we should not necessarily teach science from a moral and ethical standpoint. As Wolpert says in the quotation at the head of this chapter, science describes the world as it is, that is all that science should do he contends. Science and scientists should, in effect, be free to research any and all aspects of nature. The acquisition of knowledge and understanding is the only consideration. It is only when that knowledge is applied to problem solving should consideration of morals and ethics be considered important. Such considerations are human attributes – such considerations do not, as far as we can ascertain, apply in the non-human animal kingdom.

If we describe the life of the lions of the African savannah then we do not say that the lion is without morals and ethics because it hunts and kills, either for food or to defend its territory. We do not consider morals and ethics when we look to explain the interrelationships that exist in ecosystems. We do not apply acts of morality and ethical decisions to animals as these are uniquely human traits. In short, we should have no real need to consider morals and ethics when studying interrelationships in biology – yet we do consider just these things if we place humans somewhere in this relationship. For example human activity and its impact on ecosystems can induce discussion about the effect that humans have (in a negative way) and how we should carefully mitigate against these negative effects when planning any activity in any ecosystem. From local planning applications to stopping coastal erosion from destroying homes on cliff edges, the impact on the environment is a key consideration.

Humans also study ecosystems and this can throw up issues with a moral and ethical dimension. If a lion cub is stranded from its mother and being attacked by a leopard, a scientist observing this should not intervene and save the cub – that would be seen as unethical – you cannot interfere with 'nature' would be the justification. If the observer were carrying out research on the life of the lions of the savannah – the researcher would have to think about the ethics of what he or she was proposing to do – they would have to consider in advance certain scenarios and what they would and would not do in such situations. This may well be a set-piece scenario that the researcher would have thought through. Even if the cub was the last cub of that litter and the litter was the object of the research, saving that cub, so that the research could continue, would probably not be enough of a justification for the researcher to intervene and break some ethical code.

Let's take another, similar, scenario. What if there was a researcher looking at an extremely rare group of animals and the litter was the last-known surviving litter of that species with no other reproductively viable animals left in captivity or as far as was known, in the wild. Should the researcher find that the lives of these animals were in danger and that by not intervening that species would become extinct, what then? Should they intervene and save the cub? Perhaps you could argue that they had a moral duty to save this animal from sure fire extinction. Would breaking an ethical code which says that the researcher should not intervene be acceptable?

The concept of morals and ethics may be a uniquely human thing. Certainly animals have been shown to be caring towards each other and towards their offspring, but this is not called either a moral and ethical stance. Those two words are applied to the human condition rather than the animal condition. An argument then for teaching science from a moral and ethical standpoint could be that as humans, uniquely we have a concept of morals and ethics and it would be almost impossible for a human being (scientist) to work without any application of their own moral and ethical framework. This may be applied consciously or sub-consciously. Science may tell us how the world 'is' but cannot tell us how that knowledge should be used and applied. Being aware of moral and ethical frameworks, either personal or general, guides the application of our knowledge and understanding.

Introducing morals and ethics into science teaching

Donnelly (2004) suggests three domains where morals and ethics can be integrated into science teaching. The first concerns the ethical conduct of science itself, which includes ideas about honesty and integrity; collecting and reporting data with rigour and accuracy; avoiding plagiarism; not using the data of others without permission etc. This is not a uniquely scientific position, he argues, the same moral and ethical approach could be said to be important for the historian as well as the scientist. Donnelly argues that while teaching students about honesty and integrity is important, it can easily be achieved in other curriculum areas and it is not necessary for this to be done in science.

Donnelly's second domain is where scientific activity is concerned with phenomena that are ethically sensitive, for example the study of sentient living creatures. It may well be the case that the instances of schools keeping live animals for such studies have declined, but even with a simple activity such as collecting organisms in leaf litter or investigating the school or nearby pond/ meadow, there will be in place ethical standards about exactly what pupils can and cannot do. Science is not the only curriculum subject where such ethical protocols need to be in place. In schools where psychology is an examination subject, the idea of studying human subjects for small-scale experiments may be common. This requires a lot of attention to ethical standards. Alternatively, where pupils study history and conduct interviews of relatives or others about their memories of major historical events, such ethical considerations also need to be in place.

Donnelly's third domain relates to those issues where scientific knowledge throws up immediate and recognizable ethical questions, for example creating genetically modified organisms; use of mobile phones; global warming/ climate change. Donnelly sees this last domain as contentious because such issues, far from being peripheral to the curriculum, have now moved to be a more central driving force for curriculum reform and such ideas/subjects are now, in the light of the recent curriculum reforms, more central to how science should be taught.

These three domains provide a convenient and useful way of separating moral and ethical issues in science teaching. It may also provide a way of prioritizing teaching. While domain 1 is important, a survey of approaches and coverage in other curriculum areas may reveal that the pupils are already quite well versed in such considerations. Domain 2 may have importance if work with animals is undertaken within science and discussions about the treatment of animals and how ethics works when scientists are working with an animal or human subject will be important. Domain 3 is the most likely domain of engagement that science teachers will tackle on a day-to-day basis in teaching science.

Having established that taking a moral and ethical approach to teaching science is, in some ways, intrinsic to science education – though it may not be central to the pursuit of science itself – the question has to asked, how do we promote ethical thinking in science teaching?

Ethical thinking in science

In much the same way that we need to distinguish questions that science can and cannot answer we also need to distinguish between those questions in

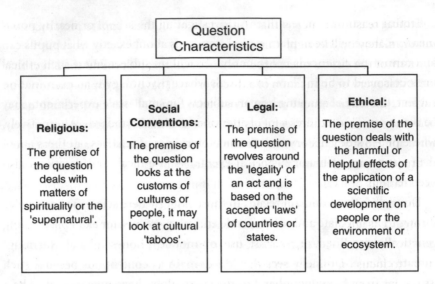

Figure 8.1 Question Characteristics adapted from Paul and Elder (2005)

science which may have an ethical dimension (and so qualify as suitable questions for engaging pupils in ethical thinking) and those that do not (see Chapter 5 for a fuller discussion on questions in science). Many interesting questions that pupils may pose in class may at first sight appear to have the look and feel of questions that address ethical or moral issues. It is useful to distinguish between questions of religion, convention and law and those which are truly ethical questions in the realm of science. The problem of course arises when ethical questions have a legal, social or religious dimension. Figure 8.1 usefully defines the characteristic of questions and how we may separate out those questions which would have an ethical dimension that could be discussed in class.

When an ethical question has been posed it is necessary to get the pupils to think about their response to the question. A problem to highlight to pupils is that we are all prone to

> egotism, prejudice, self-justification, and self-deception and that these flaws in human thinking are the cause of much human suffering. Only the systematic cultivation of fair-mindedness, honesty, integrity, self-knowledge, and deep concern for the welfare of others can provide foundations for sound ethical reasoning.
>
> (Paul and Elder, 2005: 5)

Ethical reasoning means that in the face of all these innate prejudices we will ultimately do the 'right' thing.

Many of the ethical questions in science will revolve around the effect that some discovery or application of a discovery will have on people – society – as a whole, the environment or the ecosystem. Some of these interesting questions may hinge on disagreements between scientists. Disagreements are the norm for How Science Works. In some ways they are necessary for science to proceed and for ideas to become accepted by the scientific community. Explanations of natural phenomena will only become accepted theories once the disagreements have been aired and the evidence for and against such ideas debated. Disagreement is, in some senses, actively encouraged to allow for ideas to be tested – even falsified. It can be easy however for such disagreements to focus on the person rather than the idea, so, within science, Wessel (1980) proposed the following 'rules of engagement' for disagreements in science

1. **Openness:** Data will not be withheld simply because it is deemed to be 'negative' or 'unhelpful' for the scientist's case.
2. **Disclosure:** Data should be disclosed in a timely fashion and not held to obtain any tactical advantage.
3. **Delay:** Scientists should not delay investigations/experiments as a tactic to avoid an undesired result.
4. **Motivation:** Scientists should not question the motivation of adversaries. Personal habits and characteristics will not be questioned unless relevant.
5. **Interest in an outcome:** Scientists should disclose any bias, prejudice or vested interest in their work or any significant sponsorship which could affect their judgement as a matter of course.
6. **Orderly retreat:** An opponent who disagrees with a scientist should be able to 'exit' the argument with honour.
7. **Unfair tricks:** Scientists will not employ 'tricks' designed to mislead in order to win an argument.
8. **Complex ideas** will be simplified as much as possible to achieve maximum communication and lay understanding.
9. **Effort:** Scientists should be made to make clear any uncertainties in the data or evidence and when ideas are in the form of a hypothesis this will be disclosed willingly, not reluctantly. Unjustified assumptions and off-the-cuff comments will be avoided.
10. **Extremism:** Scientists may counter any extreme views, but dogmatism will be avoided.

Examining cases from the history of science and, indeed, contemporary cases where disagreements feature, can be a useful way of engaging students. Using a moral and ethical dimension in our science teaching leads of course to the fact that we must also assess our pupils' achievement. We will need to chart their progression in ethical thinking.

Assessing science from a moral and ethical teaching standpoint

Assessing whether or not a pupil has the right or wrong answer to a question can, at first sight, seem relatively easy. Ask a pupil to name a specific bone in the leg and if the correct answer is tibia and the pupil incorrectly identifies this as the fibula, it is clear cut, the answer is wrong. Ask another pupil if we should use more nuclear power to reduce our reliance on non-renewable energy sources and there is no correct answer as such. The second question is also of a different order to the first. The first simply requires knowledge – it is something that the pupil either knows or does not know. It is, according to Bloom's Taxonomy, a low-level question (Figure 8.2). The second question requires not just knowledge but also understanding. Synthesis and evaluation are needed in order to provide a response. Providing the question in a way that just elicits a yes or no response deprives the marker of knowledge of that synthesis and evaluation. This means that how and where a question is asked is important.

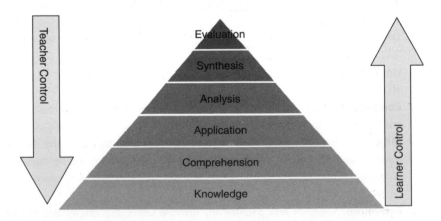

Figure 8.2 Bloom's Taxonomy – Cognitive Domain

The question, as it stands in this text, could be answered with a yes or no response. In a discussion situation this question is likely to be followed by a supplementary question asking the respondent to justify their answer – give reasons why they said yes or no. Discussion in a classroom situation is a better way of assessing the response as it provides the necessary space for follow-up questions or challenges from peers. In other words a dialogue is needed to make a fair assessment, where not just knowledge, but understanding is also required.

As a written question on the issue of nuclear power then the question above would have a number of problems, not least the tendency of pupils to provide the simplest answer – either yes or no. It is unlikely that many pupils would, unprompted, provide justification for their answer. When designing opportunities for the assessment of ethics in science it is important to allow the respondent time and space to construct a narrative or spoken response which is more than just a knee jerk reaction to a statement or which is more than a simple yes or no.

In a report on assessing ethics for the Nuffield Foundation a number of recommendations were made which included making a distinction between ethical reasoning and scientific reasoning; consideration of the demands placed on science teachers; how to recognize progression from a novice to advanced ethical thinking in students; greater time and space to provide answers to written questions and an allocation of marks that reflects the complexity of thinking necessary to provide high-level answers (Reiss, 2009: 4–6). See Figure 8.3.

Science itself is neither 'good' nor 'bad'. How that knowledge is used however can be for good or bad purposes, for example knowledge of nuclear fission and the development of the atomic bomb. Even more recent scientific discoveries, such as cloning, can have properties of 'good' and 'bad' linked to them. For example cloning plants with specific characteristics that mean they have a higher vitamin yield or resistance to pests could be argued to be a good thing. Cloning humans is considered a bad thing. The knowledge of cloning – the actual science of cloning is neither good nor bad. It is the application of a moral and ethical dimension that determines if something is good or bad.

There is a danger when considering the moral and ethical dimension of science of ignoring the basic knowledge of science. Discussion of issues such as cloning, nuclear power, mobile 'phones etc. cannot be done without some

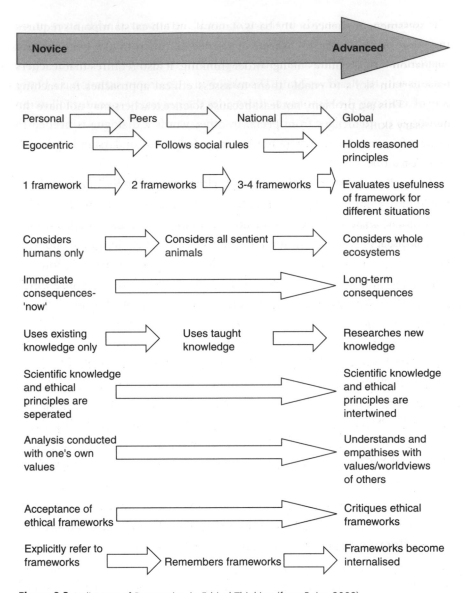

Figure 8.3 Indicators of Progression in Ethical Thinking (from Reiss, 2009)

knowledge of the science behind these issues. In order to synthesize and evaluate something you must have some knowledge and comprehension. When arguing from a point of ignorance about the science behind nuclear power or cloning you are more likely to generate misconceptions and misunderstanding.

Assessment of science on the basis of moral and ethical standpoints requires the pupils to know certain aspects of science and then to use synthesis and evaluation – this requires higher-order thinking. It also requires that teachers have certain skills to enable them to assess ethical approaches to teaching science. This is a problem, not least because science teachers may not have the necessary skills;

> It must be admitted that the present state of our education system fails to provide either teachers or pupils with the necessary skills to address this problem. Scientists grapple with it in ignorance of a sound ethical dimension and those with knowledge and skills in the ethical field are ignorant of science. In the short term there seems little we can do but continue to try to lift ourselves with our own bootstraps.
>
> (Hall, 2004: 26)

A useful model of progression that can be applied to students' ethical thinking was developed in 2007 by a New Zealand project on bioethics (Figure 8.2). In this model a range of indicators are identified that could be used to show progression in students' thinking on ethical issues. The model is not a fixed one where students will automatically progress along the axes indentified for each indicator. Students may, by the time they come to discuss such issues in secondary science, already have developed and progressed from novice towards advanced thinkers in some aspects. How quickly they will (may have) progressed will depend on a range of factors including their own interest in the topic under discussion (Jones et al., 2007; Reiss, 2009; Reiss, 2010).

Reflective task

Tackling moral and ethical issues in science can be tricky. Ideally there should be a policy and procedures which govern how such issues are tackled in the classroom. Reflect as a science team on the range and nature of the issues used in class as moral and ethical issues. Discuss any possible sensitivities and problems that could arise from the use of these issues in class and decide on any departmental policy and rules that should be in place. Has the policy, once in place, been communicated to all the stakeholders for example the pupils (so that they know the types of issues that will and won't be discussed and any rules for discussion), the parents, the senior management of the school and/or the governors?

Classroom task

In the film *Jurassic Park* scientists re-create dinosaurs from DNA extracted from blood-sucking insects trapped in amber. The science behind *Jurassic Park* is not possible today and may never be possible. One of the characters, Dr Ian Malcolm, played by Jeff Goldblum, said 'your scientists were so preoccupied with whether or not they could, they didn't stop to think if they should!'; this character was arguing that scientists should always think about the consequences of the work that they do. Imagine that the science in *Jurassic Park* was possible. Do you agree with Dr Malcolm? Just because we can re-create dinosaurs should we? Construct an argument on either moral or ethical grounds either for or against using such scientific understanding to bring back extinct species. How would you decide which species to bring back and which to not bring back?

References

Dickens, C. 2008. *Hard Times,* Oxford: Oxford University Press.

Donnelly, J. F. 2004. Ethics and the science curriculum. *School Science Review,* 86, 29–32.

Hall, E. 2004. Science and Ethics: give them a break. *School Science Review,* 86, 25–28.

Jones, A., McKim, A., Reiss, M., Ryan, B., Buntting, C., Saunders, K., De Luca, R. and Conner, L. 2007. Research and development of classroom-based resources for bioethics education in New Zealand, Hamilton: The Bioethics Council. Wilf Malcolm Institute of Educational Research, University of Waikato.

Paul, R. and Elder, L. 2005. Ethical Reasoning. Foundation for Critical Thinking. http://www.critical-thinking.org/files/SAM-EthicalReasoning20051.pdf

Reiss, M. J. 2009. *Assessing Ethics in Secondary Science,* London: Nuffield Foundation.

Reiss, M. J. 2010. Ethical Thinking. In: Jones, A., McKim, A. and Reiss, M:, J. (eds.) *Ethics in the Science and Technology Classroom: A New Approach to Teaching and Learning,* Taipei: Sense Publishers.

Wessel, M. R. 1980. *Wessel: Science and Conscience (Cloth),* New York: Columbia University Press.

Wolpert, L. 2004. *Prof Lewis Wolpert Debates Theraputic Cloning* [Online]. Y Touring Theatre Company. Available: http://www.geneticfutures.com/ltltg/info/sheet9.asp [Accessed 10 November 2009].

Wolpert, L. 2005. Life lessons. *The Guardian,* 7 April 2005.

Investigation and Experimentation in Science

9

The loveliest theories are being overthrown by these damned experiments; it's no fun being a chemist anymore.

(Justus von Liebig (1803–1873) German Chemist)

Experiments are the bread and butter of science, though are all sciences characterized by experiments? Can an astronomer really do an experiment as we normally envisage them taking place? For school science, experimentation and investigation is fundamental to teaching and learning. The reasons for taking an enquiry-based approach to science are many and various. Some revolve around the idea of engagement – practical activities can be fun and can inspire 'awe and wonder'. For others there is the idea that some students are better suited to a kinaesthetic way of learning – learning by doing – in which case practical activities are integral to engaging pupils who exhibit this preferred learning style. Practical work is also a distinctive characteristic of science as a discipline. It can be thought of as a defining characteristic for students. When asked to draw their concept of a scientist, students invariably set the scientist in the laboratory amid practical equipment and not sat at a computer, or in a library or even conducting field work gathering data (Buldu, 2006).

In their report on the future of science education, Millar and Osborne (1998) warned against the development of future curriculum models for science which were overly reliant on the traditional practical and investigative approach to science (what was known as Sc1 or 'scientific enquiry'). While they recognized its importance they also saw its limitations.

In this chapter we will look at the role of experiments and investigations in developing students' understanding of science and explore the experimental and investigative approach to science through the language that now characterizes the new GCSE specifications.

Unrealistic science

Should all scientific experiments in schools work? Although this is, at first sight, a simple question the answer is somewhat complex. Teachers spend a lot of time looking for 'foolproof' experiments that can deliver the desired result in classroom laboratories. Various 'cheats' have been used in the past to ensure the success of an otherwise unreliable experiment, from adding some sodium bicarbonate to photosynthesizing *elodea* to ensure the production of enough (some) collectable oxygen, to downright fraud where a failed experiment has some substituted data or end product which confirms the 'theory' or idea being covered in the science scheme of work. How school science relates to 'real' science is a matter that the How Science Works approach should make clear to students. 'Real science' does not have a regime where experiments regularly deliver meaningful and definite results and which may be considered as positive contributions to our knowledge and understanding of natural phenomenon. 'Real' scientists will recount how many laboratory experiments deliver negative results or simply deliver no results. This does not represent a failure of science, on the contrary, negative and 'no result' experiments have their place to play in confirming testable ideas or hypotheses.

We also promote an unrealistic view of science during our attempts in secondary school to attract pupils from our feeder primary schools. The traditional 'open evening' with its plethora of exciting science experiments involving the stereotypical school laboratory approach utilizing the best and perhaps underused equipment can lead to expectations above and beyond that which is delivered to the primary pupil once the transfer to secondary school is completed. The consequence is a cohort of pupils who may feel let down as the excitement of open evening science is replaced by the routine, less than exciting day-to-day science work, in some cases not using a practical approach for the majority of teaching time. The excitement of science is only emulated by the setting up of a science club – an after-school activity which breaks away from a restrictive curriculum to deliver 'interesting' science.

Research into practical work in science has been undertaken over many years and the importance of this research supports the view that practical work in science is a core 'deliverable' that science teachers should support. Hart (2000) summarized research into practical work in laboratories which shows that the fundamental concern of many students while in the laboratory is completion of the task, and that this concern can overwhelm any serious learning possibilities. Much of the research focuses on the purpose, use and learning that come from laboratory work. Other research cited by Hart shows that laboratory work can cognitively overload students with too many things to recall. Other studies state that small qualitative tasks can promote conceptual change. Small tasks, it was argued, aid in students' reconstructing their thinking as less time is spent on interacting with apparatus, instructions etc., and more time spent on discussion. Some researchers describe laboratory work as often being dull and teacher-directed and highlighted the fact that students often failed to relate the laboratory work to other aspects of their learning.

The language of science experiments

With the introduction of How Science Works, attention towards experimental and investigative approaches in science education took a new turn. In Chapter 4 we looked at the language associated with key aspects of the nature of science, theories, laws, hypotheses etc. At the end of the chapter I advocated the use of the prefix 'scientific' to help distinguish the common or vernacular use of terms from the more specific use of that term in a science context. Context alone, as illustrated in Chapter 4 with the sentence 'Copper is a good conductor', is often insufficient to establish the correct definition of 'copper' as a person or as the metal.

With the new examination specifications, developed with How Science Works as a driving force, came the introduction of a range of terms which characterized the practical approach to science. Terms such as accurate and precise, valid and reliable began to receive much more prominence. A summary of terms commonly associated with How Science Works and the current GCSE specifications are found in Table 9.1 and Table 9.2.

Table 9.1 Investigation terminology for How Science Works

Term	Meaning	Example
Accuracy	An accurate measurement is one which is very close to the true value	An African Elephant weighs about 7,500 kg, to make an accurate measurement you would have to measure an actual elephant.
Random error	This sort of error can cause readings to be different from the true reading.	Taking large numbers of readings can help to cancel out random errors. Just measuring once is not enough, lots of measurements are needed.
Systematic error	This type of error causes readings to be spread about and shifted one way or the other from the true value	Readings may be taken but consistently recorded incorrectly. This leads to a systematic error where the readings taken are not representative of the true value.
Zero error	This is a type of systematic error	An ammeter where the needle does not go back to zero when there is no current flowing is an example of a zero error
Fair test	In a fair test only the independent variable is allowed to affect the dependent variable	To achieve a fair test, all the other variables must be kept constant, for example if a ball drop experiment is carried out where the surfaces the ball is being dropped onto are different and the size of the ball being dropped is different, that is not a fair test
Precision	The precision of a measurement depends on the scale being used	Measuring in millimetres is more precise than using centimetres
Reliability	Measurements and results are reliable if they can be repeated	You can check reliability by comparing your results with others, or by repeating measurements and calculating the mean
True value	This is an accurate value, measured without error	Using a sophisticated and properly calibrated thermometer a temperature reading of 35 °C can be said to be a 'true' value
Validity	Data is only valid if the measurements result from a single independent variable	If measurements are taken from a test that is not fair, then the results are not valid. For example, any measurements of the height that the balls bounce in the test mentioned above are not valid because the test is not fair

Table 9.2 Terminology for Variables

Name of variable	Meaning	Example
Independent	This is the variable that you deliberately change to see what effect it has	In an experiment to investigate Hooke's Law you could use one or two masses or more to stretch the spring
Dependent	This is the variable that you measure. It is the variable that you think will change because you changed the independent variable	In Hooke's law experiment you measure the length that the spring has extended. The extension length depends on the mass
Categoric	A categoric variable has values which are described by labels	In an experiment heating different materials, the categoric variable labels could be copper, iron and glass
Continuous	These variables can have any numerical value, in other words the numbers can also have fractions/ decimals	In a Hooke's law experiment to measure how a mass stretches a spring, the length of the spring could be 15.1 cm, 15.5 cm, 15.9 cm . . . or any number in between
Discrete	These variables can only have whole numbers as values that is 1, 2, 3, . . .	In a class survey, the number of people with brown eyes is 1 or 2 or 3 etc.
Ordered	These are categoric variables that can be put into an order	In an experiment to investigate the effects of a parachute on the rate of descent, the parachute could be large, medium or small
Controlled	This is a variable or variables that you should not change, so that any test you do is a fair test	In an experiment to test how fast different liquids cool you must use the same amount of liquid in each beaker

The clear implication from looking at the language associated with the investigative and experimental side of How Science Works is that science is about such things as precision and reliability, it cannot be conducted if the tests that we use to try out our ideas are not fair and there is even a notion that science is about the pursuit of truth for example with reference to seeking the 'true' value. Science has been dominated by a practical and experimental/ investigative approach as has been noted. What we need to consider are the goals of student learning that are associated with practical work. As early as the nineteenth century a practical approach to science teaching and learning has been favoured. From very informal practical settings – such as the primary 'nature' table common over 50 years ago to whole examination courses that begin from a practical investigative approach, such as the Secondary Science Education Programme (1965–1974); the Junior Science Project (1960–1974); the Combined Science Project (1964–1970). In addition there were major developments in single sciences at A level such as the Salter's approach to sciences. Numerous other projects have tried to boost science teaching and learning with varying degrees of success. The move to How Science Works and the development of the new twenty-first-century Science specifications represent the most major change in the approach to teaching and learning science for many generations.

Goals for learning in the school laboratory

In general there is one overarching goal for situating learning in the school laboratory (or outdoors in the field) as opposed to situating it in a normal classroom. It is to promote the development of the students' scientific knowledge, problem-solving abilities and practical skills. This goal would include the development of conceptual knowledge; practical skills (from using instruments to setting up 'standard' equipment associated with laboratory work, such as Bunsen burners, tripods, stands, clamps and bosses etc); problem solving through a process of design and implementation of an experiment or experiments which provide a solution to an often real-life-based problem; gaining an understanding of how science and scientists work; to promote interest and motivation to study and further study the sciences and last, but by no means least, to gain an understanding of the methods of scientific enquiry and reasoning. It is this last goal which is in some ways the most contentious. As we have noted elsewhere, school science does not resemble 'real' science much and how science works in schools is not necessarily a good model for how science works in practice in the real world. There is also a danger that the science we practise in school laboratories is so far removed from real science that those who are encouraged to take up science post 16 and at university may soon become disillusioned by the science that they practise, just as primary pupils can become disillusioned with the science they conduct in secondary school when compared with their experience of science at the school open evening.

'Real science' utilizes new technologies at a very fast rate. School laboratories hardly have changed over the past 100 years. A 1950s science teacher could still comfortably work in the school laboratory of 2010. There are some recent technological advances that help science teaching and learning such as the advent of the World Wide Web, the internet and the use of interactive white boards. Computers are now more common in laboratories, but not on a one-to-one basis – that is still probably some way off for the majority of schools. Some practical approaches to teaching science that utilize computer animations, simulations, computer models and video/audio transmission of real time or recorded events do not need a traditional laboratory in which to teach the lesson. It could as easily be taught within a computer suite or a standard classroom. As technology advances the gulf between real research/commercial laboratories and school laboratories is bound to get bigger. Schools are, and will probably for many years be, unable to afford the levels of equipment and specialization that professional laboratories achieve, if ever. Is it time then to examine carefully the purpose of school laboratory work and to examine the benefits of this work to the pupils? Does such work really result in measurable gains in knowledge and understanding?

This is not a call for the abandonment of practical teaching in science education in our schools. Neither is it a call for less investment in time or resources to improve science teaching and learning. It is a call for rational thinking and the development of a clear purpose in what practical activities we teach, how we teach them and when those activities are best delivered.

A science education for the twenty-first century will be different from that which dominated the nineteenth and twentieth centuries. In bygone days laboratory activities tended to be learning experiences where the students interacted with materials and secondary sources in order to try and understand the natural world. There was a much more restricted curriculum that focused on the supply and demand for scientists and technologists. The approach to science education was a utilitarian one; the argument went along the lines of it *'it is necessary to teach children how to do practical experiments not for the prime purpose of illustrating ideas and concepts but more to ensure that they were aware of the practical procedures and skills necessary to fulfil a work based position which required such skills.'*

Such an argument has less of a priority today. We must acknowledge that the vast majority of our students will not progress on to post 16 and higher education in the sciences. The curriculum must therefore not be for the prime purpose of providing future scientists and technologists. It must be for the purpose of improving scientific literacy and enabling future generations to engage with science on a social level not necessarily on a functional practical level.

Already I envisage lots of science teachers reading this crying out and saying that this betrays part of what science education is about – encouraging more young people to take up science at a higher level. My response would be to encourage teachers to take on the role of identifying those students who show an aptitude for the sciences and to encourage them to study beyond the age of 16. There will necessarily be a need to look carefully at our curriculum offering and to ensure that we have sufficient choice and depth in the various options to allow those who show such an aptitude to study more content, gain greater practical skills and awareness and engage with higher-order thinking and argumentation skills so that they can carry on in their science-specific studies – for example with the provision of separate sciences that meet the needs of further science and double sciences that meet the needs of those who we wish to be scientifically literate but who we understand are not in the further science study camp. A 'one size fits all' approach will not meet the needs of society.

Where all approaches to science can benefit, is from the utilization of real science data and context in which to understand How Science Works – especially the experimental and investigative aspects. While some data are generated first hand through good practical and experimental work, this is not the only source of data that we have to hand, given the advances in information sharing and availability. Such data may come from bona-fide ongoing scientific research. Secondary sources may come from the science textbooks or, latterly, from research carried out via the internet. These sources of evidence and data may then inform the students' thinking about a concept or idea.

Virtual science

The advent of freely available 'knowledge' can however lead to teaching in such a way as to encourage the uncritical use of such material. Students have become adept at 'finding' or 'Googling' for information to the extent that their research tasks – often set as homework – are no more than 'virtual' homework.

Virtual in two senses; the data may itself be virtual data or information and the students will have done virtually nothing to the data and information before it is handed in. The key question here is who is at fault? The person who sets the homework that can be fulfilled in such a way, or the student who merely sees the easiest route to completing the task given?

The advent of powerful computers and easy access to the World Wide Web throws up interesting challenges for the teacher of science. It also affords opportunities to look again at what we envisage practical laboratory work to be, for example computer simulations and computer modelling figures large in the work of real scientists, from chemists who construct and deconstruct complex molecules to astrophysicists who model the evolutionary history of stars and galaxies. Real data is now abundant and easy to obtain. It is possible to look up the genetic data, the DNA sequences of genes and of whole organisms. DNA sequencing costs have fallen dramatically from the 100s of millions of pounds sterling it took to sequence the first human genome to the idea that every person could have their own personal genome data at a relatively cheap cost (hundreds rather than thousands of pounds sterling) within the next 10 years. Being able to access the genomes of major animal groups can help us teach the story of the development and diversity of life on earth and produce a much more meaningful story of evolution than we can at present using old and outdated examples such as the evolution of the horse. Considering the 'power' that these data have in social terms is also an excellent teaching point. Who should have access to our DNA data and how should it be controlled/used? The moral and ethical arguments that arise over such issues present us with another teaching challenge. How can we debate this issue without the knowledge of what DNA is and how DNA stores the blueprint of our lives in the form of genes? If one of the main purposes of science education is scientific literacy, then the practical approach to science teaching is to look at what DNA is, where it is found and how it works. Then come the much wider teaching objectives of considering the moral and ethical implications of understanding DNA and to realize its potential for use and misuse in society. We may start from the content, the 'science' of DNA or we may start from the social implications of who has access to our DNA but in both cases we must harmonize the content with the process of science. In this way we achieve scientific literacy.

Conclusion

There is no doubt that the practical side of science has a firm place in the curriculum of our schools. We cannot ignore the 'awe and wonder' that a reactive metals demonstration can achieve and we cannot doubt that our practical work can provide a cognitive challenge for many of those long-held and widespread misconceptions. In addition, practical science can deliver more than just a fun lesson, end of term entertainment or a rest from the 'serious' academic stuff. Practical science if envisioned and enacted carefully can support and enhance so much of what we set out to achieve in science teaching and learning. It can deliver practical skills, it can promote thinking skills and it can corroborate scientific theory and practice. Its place needs careful consideration in the framework of How Science Works as we seek to establish a new order for science teaching – away from the dominant fact-based transmission of knowledge, to a new era of process skills in science that value the thinking approach and argumentation as much as the history and philosophy of science. Experimentation and investigation must now seek to establish its role in the new framework. This means moving away from the idea that experimentation and investigation is the prime goal of How Science Works to the idea that it is one part of a mutually supportive framework of interconnected spheres that make up what happens in 'real' science beyond the science classroom.

Reflective task

Look carefully at the definitions of HSW terminology expressed in your current specifications and review your resources to ensure that there is consistency in the use and definition of terminology. Consider how and when the terms are introduced and the examples used to illustrate the term. Decide if a worksheet which explains the terminology could be produced for all pupils to ensure consistency in their use.

References

Buldu, M. 2006. Young children's perceptions of scientists: a preliminary study. *Educational Research*, 48, 121–132.

Hart, C., Mulhall, P., Berry, A., Loughran, J. and Gunstone, R. 2000. What is the purpose of this experiment? Or can students learn something from doing experiments? *Journal of Research in Science Teaching,* 37, 655–675.

Millar, R. and Osborne, J. 1998. Beyond 2000: Science Education for the Future. London: King's College.

10 Communicating Science

```
┌──────────────────────────────────────────────────────────┐
│                                                            │
│   Chapter Outline                                          │
│                                                            │
```
```
└──────────────────────────────────────────────────────────┘
```

Reading maketh a full man; conference a ready man and writing an exact man.

(Francis Bacon (1561–1626) Philosopher of Science)

Scientists do not begin their work by thinking about how they may present their findings to the general public. Much less do they think about making their language accessible or understandable. When their work is finally picked up and presented by the media, it is most often done by a press release which is likely to be written by someone who is a journalist rather than a scientist. Scientists then complain that their findings are distorted, glamorized, misrepresented or are just plain wrong. Whose fault is it? And how should scientists communicate their findings? This is a part of How Science Works that is particularly important for our students. They will be the receivers of scientific communication whether they like it or not. They will watch and listen to the news, read the newspapers and be subject to influence by the media. Communicating science in the media is just one aspect of scientific communication that you need to consider when presenting How Science Works to your students. To appreciate How Science works, or more importantly how scientists work, students must gain an understanding of the process of communicating science to the community of scientists and the general public. Knowing the procedures for communicating new ideas also helps them to understand aspects of the reliability and validity of what they are reading. As well as communicating the work in a written format, scientists will also give lectures (academic and public) about their work and discoveries and may find themselves being interviewed on television and radio. Some scientists are now making their own television and radio series to promote and aid scientific communication. Writing for all these different audiences takes skill and an understanding of the medium through which the communication is being provided. While professional scientists will have developed certain skills, for example how to write an academic paper or a technical report, they may not be able to write a 600-word newspaper article or be able to present their ideas in a two-minute television broadcast.

How is science communicated?

Science is communicated to a range of audiences in a variety of ways. Each method of communication has its own protocols and procedures and each its own purpose. We can helpfully split the methods up as follows:

- Technical Communication
- Academic Communication
- Professional Communication
- Everyday Communication

Each method will have distinct target audiences and particular 'rules' for generating the communication (e.g. technical papers must follow particular patterns for how they are written, from the broad content areas down to the method of referencing the work of others). Each audience will also have its own expectations of what the communication should do – for example readers of a newspaper are not interested in the results of scientific endeavour unless there is either some element of usefulness to them or to society, or an aspect of 'awe and wonder' – for example the discovery of a previously unknown giant dinosaur or human ancestor or the development of a new 'wonder drug' (a phrase which has its own problems in what is being conveyed to the reader).

Technical communication

Most technical communication is done through reports, such as evaluations of or instructions for repeating experiments or processes. This aspect of communication is a necessary part of scientific communication. It is not the sort of communication that the lay person will read and it will not be of use to delve too deeply into technical reports and report writing while considering How Science Works. In schools, writing up investigations or experiments is as close to technical report writing as most students will get. In this genre, the writing can be staid and uninteresting and will not appeal to a wide audience. People read technical reports because they have to rather than that they want to read them for pleasure.

These types of reports will be very specific, detailed and factual, contain graphics that are informative rather than decorative and in some cases can run to hundreds of pages. Technical reports in science are like the manuals that accompany gadgets or cars. People don't often read them – preferring to go straight to the 'quick start guide', but sometimes find that the level of detail provided in such reports is needed when a problem arises.

Scientists, like technologists and others, may well have to write technical reports for their experiments or processes, they are never the first things written – often only being compiled once the experiment or process is established and confirmed, but at some point every scientific discovery needs a technical report of some type.

Academic communication

This is the commonest form of communication by scientists of their work. In general, science is disseminated by way of academic publishing. As a scientist makes discoveries or adds new evidence to already existing ideas, academic paper writing is the mode of communication preferred. The process of writing and publishing academic papers may well take up more time for scientists than working in their laboratories running, devising or repeating experiments. Publication of work is very important for the scientist or group of scientists working on a problem or idea. By publishing, scientists can lay claim to priority for ideas; they set out questions and answers and inform the community of scientists of their progress. More importantly their ideas are subject to peer review – an essential component for getting ideas accepted by the scientific community (see below for a more detailed discussion of the peer review process).

Maintaining a good publishing record is also important for career progression for scientists. For example, in university work, progression from post-doctoral researcher to lecturer climbing to the acquisition of a Chair (Professor) in your field requires you to publish work at an internationally recognized level which could be seen as 'world leading'. Writing any old thing in any old publication will not be sufficient. Academics – which includes many working research scientists – will only wish to publish in journals that are recognized as leading journals in their field.

Not all professional scientists work at universities however and many will be employed by large national and international organizations. Publication in academic journals will still be a goal for communicating their work to the scientific community, but technical reports and professional publications may be more the means of day-to-day communication.

Professional communication

While academic publication is the core means of communicating ideas within the scientific professions, many academics and scientists working in industry will undertake to communicate their findings through professional means. Often this will entail attending conferences arranged by the industry within which they work to talk about their findings and the technical details of their discoveries – making sure of course to protect the commercial side of their work with patents and other legal protection measures. Some conferences will also be academic as well as professional and many scientists will belong to professional bodies which will provide magazines and outlets where they can communicate to others interested in their field. Many professional journals will be peer reviewed, but the standard of writing and standard of referencing will be less than that required for academic journals. To provide a science education analogy – the International Journal of Science Education is an academic journal which is peer reviewed and the standard of writing which would include aspects of the methodology used in any reported research is much higher than for the School Science Review, a professional journal published by the Association for Science Education (ASE) – the professional body for science teachers. Articles here are still subject to peer review, but the standards are less onerous than for the academic journals.

Everyday communication

This is possibly the most contentious area of communication for scientists, yet it is the most common way in which the students and the general public will hear about scientific developments and new discoveries. The starting process for this form of communication is most likely to be a press release from the organization that employs the scientist. The press release will be constructed by a press or publicity officer in conjunction with the scientist or team of scientists and will attempt to make the science interesting and accessible. It will inevitably focus on some aspect which the general public will find appealing – such as a step closer to a cure for cancer or some other common ailment. It will focus on people and the impact on people rather than the technical details of the science (often there will be different press releases prepared for different audiences – technical, professional, everyday).

The common complaint from scientists and a source often of their unwillingness to engage with the press, is that it is very difficult if not impossible to convey their ideas in non-technical language in 300 words or less. Some of this will stem from their training in writing technical and academic papers. An average academic paper can be between 3,000 and 6,000 words long. The average newspaper article for a broadsheet newspaper is about 1,200 with 300–600 words for the average daily tabloid paper. It is easy to see that being asked to produce a simple, concise explanation of work that may have taken some years to complete in 600 words or less is a real struggle for many professional scientists.

The production of concise intelligible newspaper articles is the domain of the professional journalist. The mantra that accompanies the approach to good journalistic writing is derived from a 1902 Rudyard Kipling poem;

> I keep six honest serving-men
> (They taught me all I knew);
> Their names are What and Why and When
> And How and Where and Who.

At the heart of good journalistic writing are people – either the people who make the discoveries (the scientists) or the impact on people that the discovery will/may have. Simply writing about the science does not get people to read the story. This is at odds with the informal yet often followed rules of scientific writing – which is to make the writing impersonal – to remove the person from the science almost to act as if the science were completely independent of humans and human activity. Although in our writing of science in schools we have introduced the human element, there is still a tendency for science teachers to err towards reports and experimental write ups that avoid the use of the personal pronoun. Thirty years ago science teachers would severely criticize a lab report which had a statement like this '*my friend Billy and me picked up the equipment and Billy measured out 100g of copper sulphate.*' While this style may not be overtly criticized by science teachers today (though I would hope that they would pick up and correct the ungrammatical 'Billy and me') many science graduates are still taught that use of the personal pronoun is not 'good scientific writing'. Where this originates is uncertain but from the earliest days of the commonly acknowledged scientific revolution, Francis Bacon urged the use of objectivity as a sign of good science. That objectivity can easily be seen to be achieved by removing the researcher from the research. By avoiding the use of 'I' and 'me' the scientist is being objective – reporting on their findings, not bringing in any bias. This style of writing will provide certain inevitabilities to the results being communicated.

The following extract comes from an online guide to writing scientific articles:

> As a general rule, minimize your use of personal pronouns (e.g. we, our), since these can reduce the objectivity of a scientific paper. The reader already knows who has done the work. Only when it is unclear who performed the work described, such as at the end of the introduction (where you go from quoting other studies to describing your present study), should you use personal pronouns.
>
> (Anon.)

This clash of styles causes problems for scientists who wish to communicate their findings themselves, hence the need for the journalist.

The numbers of scientifically qualified journalists working in general news, either in the broadcast or print media are small. Even if a journalist does have a science qualification, this may only be to an initial degree level and will be in one limited field of science. It is unsurprising therefore that sometimes the press gets the science wrong.

Peer review

The commonality between academic and professional writing and communication is the peer review process. While all published writing – except for personal internet writing/blogs and vanity publishing – is reviewed at some stage by either an editor or sub-editor, the peer review process is somewhat different. The essence of the peer review is that anything published is deemed worthy of publication by a panel of experts in the field. The idea is quite simple. A scientist writes an article and submits this to a journal. This article is then read by two, three sometimes more, experts in the field who decide on the quality of the article and whether it is worthy of publication in that journal. The process can be open, fair and rigorous. The peer review process will vary from journal to journal but the general procedure takes the following steps.

1. A paper is submitted (mostly this is an online electronic submission procedure though printed and posted manuscripts are still accepted by many journals) and logged in the editorial system.
2. The article is sent to an Associate Editor for initial screening and to select possible reviewers, if that is judged appropriate. An associate editor may reject an article at this stage if it is clear that the article does not conform to the journal's subject matter, writing guidelines or is simply so poorly written it does not need a reviewer to point out the problems.
3. Reviewers are contacted to see if they are able to undertake a review of the article in a given timescale. Reviewers will either accept or decline the invitation
4. The review can take up to a month (or more) and is returned to the Associate Editor when complete.
5. Once the reviews from all the reviewers are received, the Associate Editor communicates the results to the original author.
6. Most articles require some further work – based on the suggestions and recommendations of the reviewers.
7. The revised article is re-submitted and often this is sent out again to the original reviewers so that they can see how the article has been changed or revised in light of their comments.
8. If there is a recommendation to accept the article, then it goes into the production process.

A key feature of the peer review process is that it should be anonymous. The author of the article does not know who is reviewing the article. In some instances the field within which the scientist works is so small that it is inevitable that they could guess who may be asked to review their work. Most journals also publish a list of their associate and assistant editors or the main reviewers and an author may be able to guess the identity of a reviewer. Sometimes, where there is disagreement between the reviewers or where the author disagrees with a reviewer's comments and criticisms, an extra opinion is sought. This extra opinion will inevitably delay the publication process. Very few articles are so well written, so well evidenced and produced that no revision is necessary.

The peer review process is, as stated, mostly anonymous. This can extend to the author of the article as well as the reviewer. Some journals prefer a review process where the author is not known to the reviewers and vice versa. Despite there being in place sophisticated mechanisms for peer review the system is not without criticism. The recent climate change controversy that erupted when e-mails from the University of East Anglia Climatic Research Unit were leaked to the press highlighted concerns about the peer review process (Pearce, 2010). The criticisms stem mainly from the fact that scientists who review the work of others may feel aggrieved if that work is criticizing their own work or standpoint on an issue. There have been calls that question the peer review process, stating that it is most likely to lead only to work that confirms previous work and which conforms to the views and ideas of the panel of reviewers (Pearce, 2010).

There is also the idea that scientists are all 'above board' and will not intend to deceive journals, their employers or others when they do their work and write about their ideas. Scientists are nearly all honest and do not intend to deceive others. This is not a firm, 100 per cent, cast iron guarantee. There have been cases where scientists have been mistaken, come to the wrong conclusion and have published in error about their work or findings. Yet others have misinterpreted or exaggerated their findings, but intentional deceit is rare. Scientists may also promote controversial ideas which go against the perceived wisdom of the current scientific community, but provided those ideas are supported by evidence then peer review should promote well-written, well-evidenced articles regardless of their own personal views. The criticism of the peer review process is, however, that some scientists may actually seek to stifle alternative views or criticisms of their work.

The criteria on which articles are judged vary from journal to journal, but generally fall into nine categories as identified by Bornmann and his co-workers (2008).

1. Relevance of contribution;
2. quality of writing;
3. experimental or research design;
4. methodological approach / statistical analysis;
5. discussion of results;
6. reference to the literature and documentation;
7. theory;
8. author's reputation / institutional affiliation
9. ethics.

Each of these categories is important for ensuring the reliability and validity of the article under consideration and should result in articles being published that are credible and withstand wider scrutiny. As has been stated, the peer review process is not without its critics and is not free from controversy. Occasionally articles get through the peer review process and are published that are flawed or contain data which are incorrect or even 'made up'. The problem is that those who undertake reviews of new and original scientific articles are not looking for deceit or dishonesty. They tend to trust that those who work in the scientific community are, on the whole, honest and do not set out to deceive. The only option open, when articles are published which subsequently turn out to be based on incorrect or fabricated data, is to retract the article.

The case of the stem cell fraud

Professor Hwang Woo-Suk was a professor of veterinary science and a researcher at Seoul University in Korea. He was a researcher who worked in the field of animal cloning and stem cell research.

Professor Hwang was, until 2006, considered to be a pioneer and leading expert in the science of cloning and stem cell research. As early as 1999 he published claims of having cloned a cow, though this was not backed, it seems, with full scientific data. He was a researcher who was able to write papers of sufficient quality to be accepted by high-profile scientific journals such as *Science*. In 2004 and 2005 he published articles that claimed he had succeeded in creating human embryonic stem cells by cloning. This was important research and the ability to clone human embryonic stem cells was of worldwide medical importance. If his claim was true it would mean that many people would benefit from custom-created treatments derived from the patient's own stem cells, thus avoiding any immune reaction problems. It transpired that Hwang had fabricated his data and the stem cell lines that he claimed to have created did not in fact exist. At this point he had been promoted to very senior positions in institutions, most of which he resigned from once his fraudulent papers had been uncovered.

The papers published in *Science* were retracted by the journal.

Good science

The goal of the peer review process is to produce good science, the best possible science. The peer review process is not perfect, but at present it is the best system in place to ensure that high standards of scientific research and publication are maintained. As the science filters down from the academic and technical papers to the professional magazines and journals to everyday newspapers, there is often a dilution of the message and many of the technical points. This dilution and, the omission of data, can be a source of frustration to the scientist, but is necessary if you wish the science to be communicated to the general public. For this to happen, we not only need good science communicators but communicators who understand science. Ultimately we need the consumers of this diluted science to understand the processes of science and how science is communicated as well as how the science goes through rigorous channels before it is accepted. To be critical, the reader needs to know what questions to ask of the article they are reading to understand how reliable and valid its contents are.

Bad science

When the press gets science wrong – as it will do from time to time – correcting the mistakes can take a lot of effort with, sometimes, little actual benefit.

Once the incorrect message is 'out' trying to put it back into a box and release the correct message can be very difficult. One scientist who campaigns against the poor reporting of good science is Dr Ben Goldacre, a medical doctor who writes a column in the Guardian Newspaper called 'Bad Science'. He also has a web presence and blog at www.badscience.net where, in his own words he *specialises in unpicking dodgy scientific claims made by scaremongering journalists, dodgy government reports, evil pharmaceutical corporations, PR companies and quacks'* (Goldacre). His book, *Bad Science,* provides a number of good illustrations about the complexities of communicating science through the media. It can be easy however to conclude that all science is poorly communicated in the media and that there is a 'hidden agenda' behind every announcement of a drug breakthrough. This simply is not the case. An interesting exercise though is to compare the reports of the same scientific 'breakthrough' or story from a range of sources from the internet to published newspapers and professional articles.

Conclusion

How science is communicated seems, at first sight, to be unproblematic. Scientists write academic articles which are published, after rigorous peer review, in respected journals and these are sometimes reported in newspaper articles. One of the aims of teaching our students about How Science Works is to enable students to engage critically with how science is communicated in the newspapers. By understanding the process that scientists have to go through to get their work accepted by the community of scientists students will be able to judge the quality of scientific evidence with which they are being presented. Should the newspaper article state that the story is based on work published in journals such as *Nature* or *Science* – then there is an indication that the science has been through the process of peer review. If the story does not make any reference to a publication in the academic literature, it is not an immediate sign that the science is suspect, but it should raise the question of whether or not this is just an opinion rather than a substantiated claim.

Key questions that need to be asked by anyone reading about any new scientific discovery or any new development should be:

1. Who is the scientist – what are their credentials?
2. What are they claiming – what evidence is being presented?

3. Where was the work carried out – for example is it a reputable institution?
4. When was the original research published and where?
5. Why is the claim/story important – how does it affect me, or society?
6. How confident can I be that the journalist has correctly interpreted the scientists work?

Kipling is not just a useful source of reminders for how to write a good story, his 'six honest men' are also useful when analysing those stories.

Reflective task

Look at back-articles of 'Bad Science' and link some of these to units of work planned for teaching aspects of How Science Works. Think about the examples as starter activities or plenaries. Think also about differentiation. Some are useful for KS3 others for GCSE or A level.

Classroom task

Ask your pupils to imagine living in an era where global communications were not available, not even the printed word. Ask them to think of a scientific idea and how they could pass this on to their friends and family in the form of a story, poem or song. What difficulty does this present in 'communicating' science?

References

Anon. Inter-Biotec: Scientific writing style.

Bornmann, L., Nast, I. and Daniel, H.-D. 2008. Do editors and referees look for signs of scientific misconduct when reviewing manuscripts? A quantitative content analysis of studies that examined review criteria and reasons for accepting and rejecting manuscripts for publication. *Scientometrics*, 77, 415–432.

Goldacre, B. *Bad Science* [Online]. Available: http://www.badscience.net/ [Accessed 12 November 2009].

Pearce, F. 2010. Climate change emails between scientists reveal flaws in peer review. *Guardian*.

Snow, C. P. 1993. *The Two Cultures*, Cambridge: Cambridge University Press.

11

How Scientists Work

As we cannot use physician for a cultivator of physics, I have referred to him as a Physicist. We need very much a name to describe a cultivator of science in general. I should incline to call him a Scientist. Thus we might say that as an Artist is a Musician, Painter, or Poet, a Scientist is a Mathematician, Physicist, or Naturalist.

(Whewell, 1858: 338)

The coining of the term 'scientist' is attributed to William Whewell (1794–1866). Prior to Whewell's use of the term scientist, those who practised science were often referred to as 'Natural Philosophers' or 'Men of Science'. Whewell was a very influential figure in nineteenth-century science, contributing more than just the word scientist – to the discipline as a whole. He was a founding member of the British Association for the Advancement of Science (BAAS) and one of its early presidents. He was a member of various famous and influential scientific societies, for example the Royal Society, a president of the Geological Society and he was Master of Trinity College, Cambridge. His influence was acknowledged by the major scientists of the day, such as Charles

Darwin, Charles Lyell and Michael Faraday. For Faraday he invented the terms 'anode', 'cathode', and 'ion'.

In this chapter we will look at how scientists work and some past controversies in science. It is tempting sometimes to think of 'science' and 'scientists' as being just one thing. As we have seen already, there are a number of disciplines that form 'science' as a whole and scientists work in many and varied ways to achieve their goals of understanding the natural world and universe.

Orchestral science

How scientists work can be envisioned by thinking of an orchestra. Science is like the played musical score. It consists of many inter-related parts, which can also operate independently, just like the sections of the orchestra (where a string quartet or a brass band can be independent or part of the whole). In its classical form, science and the orchestra produce a harmonious product; for science these are the laws, principles and theories that describe and explain natural phenomena. In orchestral terms it is the symphony or performance. Each member of the orchestra knows his or her part, understands how to produce the desired effect and can 'play' the music to achieve what the composer wanted, even though they may not be able to play all the instruments. The chemist, the physicist, the biologist etc. each knows his or her discipline and understands basically how they contribute to the whole without necessarily being experts in all disciplines. Science differs of course in that there is no 'composer' who pre-sets the outcome, who writes the score. There is no pre-written scientific score. Each branch of science and each scientist need to compose their own score from the observations, experiments and understanding they gain of the world around them. The scientists then have not only to gather and read the 'music' (in this analogy, the natural world is the music, each note being analogous to a data point, an observation, an experimental result, a deduction or an inference), they also have to figure out how these notes go together. Different scientists are like different instrumentalists. What instrument they play (their discipline) determines how they play it (their 'scientific method'). The percussionist reads their score differently from the string section whose method of producing music is quite different from the wind section.

To conceive of science or a scientist as more or less one thing is a mistake. The skills of the science teacher are often assumed to be multidisciplinary – a science teacher teaches science, so whether that is biology, chemistry, physics, geology, astronomy, psychology etc. matters not to those who timetable 'science' in the mainstream secondary school. Appreciation that different knowledge sets and skills are required is acknowledged for post 16 teaching, but lower down the school the scientist has to be all things to all people. This is like asking a musician to be able to play every instrument in the orchestra and be able to teach students how to do this. It is acknowledged that we often need to employ specialist staff to teach specific instruments to students in schools – so much so that schools limit which instruments are available for students to learn on the basis of the available peripatetic teachers. It is understood that it is not always possible to offer tuition for any and every instrument that a child may wish to play.

Recent concerns over the lack of specialists teaching physics and chemistry in schools have prompted, in part, funding towards the STEM (Science, Technology, Engineering and Maths) agenda. Recruitment into teacher education now focuses on subject knowledge and providing enhancement courses to produce more chemistry, maths and physics teachers. There are still fundamental problems that we must overcome however about how science is perceived by the public and students. Science is not one discipline, with one method, with one way of working. It requires, like an orchestra, different approaches, different skills and different knowledge bases. It may well be that how students and the general public perceive scientists needs to be challenged more.

The portrayal of scientists in the media

In Chapter 1 I briefly outlined what students think about if you ask them the simple question 'what does a scientist look like?', you will most likely get a stereotypical response which describes a balding, middle-aged, spectacle-wearing absent-minded professor. Give this question to an older, wider audience – the general public – and the most likely responses will include the child's stereotype; the mad professor bent on world domination; even the scientist as a saviour of mankind, who eliminates the virus threatening to kill all life on earth. Stereotypes will still be very prominent. The scientist for many people is at once the saviour and destroyer of mankind. The scientist is also deemed to work mainly in the laboratory, with the tools of science being glassware, Bunsen burners and bubbling coloured liquids.

Many of these stereotypes originate from media portrayals of scientists. How scientists are portrayed in the media has been investigated by Haynes (1994: 3–4) who proposed the following categories for depictions of scientists:

- **Alchemist:** a person who appears at critical times, an obsessed or maniacal scientist.
- **Stupid virtuoso:** a person who is out of touch with the real world, who can be both comic and sinister, the absent-minded professor.
- **Unfeeling person:** this is one of the most enduring stereotypes. The scientist who has reneged on human relationships, often seen as the price a person must pay to achieve scientific prowess.
- **Heroic adventurer:** who operates in the physical or intellectual world and emerges at times of scientific optimism.
- **Scientist as helpless:** the person who has lost control over their discovery or over the direction of its implementation.
- **Scientist as idealist or world saviour:** an acceptable scientist who sometimes holds out the possibility of a scientifically sustained utopia, but who often is engaged in conflict with a technology-based system that fails to provide for individual human values.

Haynes explained these categorizations of scientists as, in part, a representation of societal attitudes towards science as a discipline at the time of depiction. The characterization of scientists as unable to control their discoveries – harmful, mutated viruses that threaten human civilization, or technological developments that acquire an artificial intelligence and turn against their creators (the premise for the *Terminator* series of films and countless others) – is common and damaging to science today, even though the reality of what science can achieve and what damage science has actually done to society is far from the Hollywood creation. Science education needs to play its part in repairing this damage, but effecting such a major repair to an image that Haynes traces back to Biblical texts and Scandinavian mythology will not be easy. As she states '. . . *from the middle ages to the twentieth century, scientists as depicted in literature have, with very few exceptions, been rated as "low" to "very low" on the moral scale*' (Haynes, 1994: 4). Print and newer forms of media, film, television, videogames etc. have the greatest influence on how science is communicated to students beyond the classroom (Cresswell et al., 2009) and for this reason alone, steps must be taken to combat the stereotypes such media present.

These negative stereotypes do not go unchallenged. Meredith (2010a, 2010b) looked at the incidences of scientists in Hollywood films and recorded six times more 'hero' scientists than villainous ones. The popular demand for science-led TV programmes, such as 'CSI' and 'Waking the Dead' also provides a positive view of the work of forensic scientists. Ever popular medical programmes such as *Casualty* and *Holby City* can positively promote science. While it is right to see such moves in the films and TV as positive, one has to wonder how realistic they are as portrayals of the day-to-day life of scientists. Do forensic pathologists interrogate witnesses and solve crimes with hardly any recourse to the police? Do patients recover that quickly from major surgery as the *Holby City* patients seem to do? Is the death rate in hospitals as high as that seen in *Casualty*?

Since Haynes published her work on scientists as villains, it is indeed possible to track changes in the positive portrayal of scientists and perhaps this is linked to the increasingly diverse scientific and technological developments that infiltrate our everyday lives from the internet to mobile 'phone technology and the advent of mammalian cloning and stem cell research that promises so many positive developments in medical science.

If the stereotype does still exist, and in students it may well be more persistent than in adults, it needs to be challenged by providing alternative characterizations of scientists, in the form of real-life examples, which are meaningful to students and which represent real science and scientists. Students must understand how science works in real life so that distinctions can be drawn easily between the fictional characterizations that abound in books, plays and films etc. and how scientists really function. Understanding the work of scientists necessarily involves understanding the language of science and how science-related terminology, which may have a vernacular meaning, can also have a specific, yet different, meaning when used in a scientific context (see Chapters 4 and 9). Understanding the language of science, the methods that scientists use to gain knowledge and understanding of nature, also needs an appreciation of the history and philosophy of science. Science proceeds often by argument, by inference, by induction and by deduction.

How scientists really work

Understanding the process of science needs an appreciation of the roots of science and how science came to be the way it is today. For this reason, examining historical accounts of major developments and controversies in science and comparing these to our current understanding can be useful in showing how scientists operate (see Chapter 2). The rest of this chapter will look at some key discoveries across different disciplines to illustrate how scientists made their discoveries and how controversy was resolved.

Biology

Endosymbiosis and the acceptance of rejected science

A common misconception about science is that scientists do not like dissent or ideas that diverge from current 'accepted science'. The essence of science though is explanation of the natural world. The only constraint on the explanation is that it must be supported by evidence.

The cell is incredibly complex. Its constituent parts, its biochemistry, its role as the basic functional unit of living organisms mean that it has been a source of scientific investigation for hundreds of years. The cell was so named by Robert Hooke (1635–1703) after observing the empty box-like structures in cork. He likened them to the cells that the monks inhabited, small, relatively empty boxes. What Hooke could not have known when he published his book *Micrographia* in 1665 was that the term he used, cell, was actually going to describe not the incredibly simple, but the incredibly complex.

Little was known about the cell for almost 200 years. Then, in 1839, Theodor Schwann (1810–1882) and Matthias Jakob Schleiden (1804–1881) described the idea that plants and animals are made of cells. They put forward the notion that cells are the common unit of structure and development, in living organisms. The revolutionary idea at the heart of cell theory is that new cells come from pre-existing cells. Prior to cell theory, spontaneous generation of life was commonly accepted. Louis Pasteur and Francisco Redi challenged this orthodoxy, but it was Schleiden and Schwann's cell theory that established the cell as the functional unit of life.

The interior of the cell, the structure and function of intracellular parts, needed technology to provide the tools for investigating such minute structures. Hooke's microscope could resolve that the cell as a unit existed, but the technology of the day could not peer deep inside the cell. It took until the 1930s and the development of the electron microscope to be able to see cell organelles. Cell organelles such as chloroplasts in plants, mitochondria in plants and animals have extremely important functions in eukaryotic cells. How these organelles originated was the subject of a controversial scientific paper written by a young biologist in 1966.

Lynn Margulis (b.1938) is an evolutionary biologist who had a revelation. As a young postdoctoral researcher in the 1960s she worked on evolutionary biology from a microbial perspective rather than the normal palaeontological perspective. Her path to science came not by reading science textbooks, but classical texts by famous scientists. Having attended Chicago University at the age of 14, she graduated with a BA in liberal arts. Here she met the astronomer Carl Sagan, whom she married when she was 19. After graduation she moved to the University of Wisconsin and gained a Masters degree in zoology and genetics in 1960. Rather than be proclaimed a neo-Darwinist, she held a strict Darwinist view of evolution. Neo-Darwinism brought together the evolutionary theory of Charles Darwin (1809–1882) and Alfred Russel Wallace (1823–1913) where the mechanism was natural selection, with Mendelian Genetics – how natural selection worked at the level of DNA, something that neither Wallace nor Darwin would live to see or understand. Margulis had a problem with neo-Darwinism, which holds that variation comes from mutation. As early as the 1920s it was found that X-rays increase mutation rates in the fruit-fly. Even when fruit flies are isolated completely from X-rays and other environmental factors that could increase mutation rates, there is a spontaneous mutation rate that can be measured. Inherited variants appear spontaneously; these variants do not appear only when they are advantageous to the organism, deleterious ones will appear as well. Neo-Darwinists claimed, with evidence, that mutation was the source of variation. It was this that natural selection acted upon.

The problem that Margulis had was that even if you conducted large numbers of experiments which exposed fruit-flies to X-rays you would certainly get dead fruit-flies and perhaps fruit-flies that exhibited new variants as a result of mutation, but you would not get new species of fly. The question she posed was *'where does the useful variation upon which selection acts originate?'*

Her answer was that rather than come directly or solely from mutation the variation may come from biological mergers.

The essence of Margulis's idea was that certain cellular organelles arose not by means of mutation and natural selection, but by incorporation. So chloroplast and mitochondria, she claimed, were originally bacteria which had been ingested by early eukaryotic cells, but survived cellular digestion, becoming permanent residents of the host cell, dividing within it and providing it with energy from aerobic metabolism. Gradually, over millions of years, the endosymbionts transferred most of their genes to the host nucleus, becoming completely dependent on the host cells. The host cells, in turn, came to depend on the symbiont for aerobic energy production.

A similar process happened in plants where an ancestor of the modern green algae and plants would have ingested a cyanobacterium capable of photosynthesis. Gradually this endosymbiont also lost most of its genes to the nucleus and became dependent on the host cell, while providing the host with energy from photosynthesis. The resulting organelles are self-replicating, like the original symbiont.

Margulis wrote out her ideas and her paper was published in the *Journal of Theoretical Biology* under her married name, Sagan (1967). Her ideas were not initially accepted by the scientific community as she noted,

> In 1966, I wrote a paper on symbiogenesis called 'The Origin of Mitosing [Eukaryotic] Cells,' dealing with the origin of all cells except bacteria. (The origin of bacterial cells is the origin of life itself.) The paper was rejected by about fifteen scientific journals, because it was flawed; also, it was too new and nobody could evaluate it. Finally, James F. Danielli, the editor of the *Journal of Theoretical Biology*, accepted it and encouraged me. At the time, I was an absolute nobody, and, what was unheard of, this paper received eight hundred reprint requests. Later, at Boston University, it won an award for the year's best faculty publication. I was only an instructor at the time, so my Biology Department colleagues reacted to the commotion and threw a party. But it was more of 'Isn't this cute,' or 'It's so abstruse that I don't understand it, but others think it worthy of attention.' Even today most scientists still don't take symbiosis seriously as an evolutionary mechanism. If they were to take symbiogenesis seriously, they'd have to change their behavior. The only way behavior changes in science is that certain people die and differently behaving people take their places.
>
> (Brockman, 1996: 135)

Although her paper was published in 1966, as she stated in the quotation above, 30 years later, it was not universally accepted. Expanding on her original paper, correcting the flaws and gathering more evidence, took her 10 years of work and her resultant book, *Origin of Eukaryotic Cells* established her idea of endosymbiosis.

The story of the acceptance of endosymbiosis is useful for How Science Works as it shows how the process of science is not a straightforward path from idea to acceptance. Scientific ideas need to be communicated to the community of scientists. Original ideas may be subject to suspicion and resistance. Ideas need evidence and the greater and more robust the evidence the more likely they are to be accepted. Publication, even in a peer reviewed, respected journal is not an indication of acceptance in the scientific community as a whole – merely a forum for other scientists to discuss your ideas and look at how your research was carried out, how strong your evidence is and it allows for others to try and falsify your ideas.

Major new ideas take time to be accepted. It took Margulis 10 years of research after her first paper to produce her book on the subject and even 30 odd years later full acceptance of the idea is not guaranteed.

Geology

The asteroid extinction hypothesis

What killed the dinosaurs? Although it is now accepted generally that the end of the dinosaur era was brought about by an asteroid impact, this is a relatively recent and, in some scientific arenas, still contested idea. Did the era of the dinosaurs end with a whimper or a bang? Mass extinctions have only been subject to real scientific scrutiny for the past 30 years or so. Until the 1980s, the science of geology had a reputation for being the science that embraced fully the idea of slow change. The term 'uniformitarianism' was much bandied about as the 'way' in which geology proceeded. Uniformitarianism was an idea popularized by one of the fathers of geology, Charles Lyell (1797–1875) whose series of books, *Principles of Geology*, published between 1830 and 1833, influenced a great many scientists, including Charles Darwin. Indeed it was Lyell who co-presented Darwin's and Wallace's ideas on evolution, with Joseph Dalton Hooker (1817–1911) to the Linnean Society, London in 1858, having warned Darwin about the work of Alfred Russel Wallace and how close his ideas were to Darwin's own.

The principle of Uniformitarianism is quite simple, if not elegant. It can be summed up in one sentence; *'the present is the key to the past'*. Processes happening today are similar, if not the same, as processes that have happened in the past. The term uniformitarianism was coined by William Whewell. The idea of uniformitarianism goes back much further. It contrasts with another view of geology, that of catastrophism – yet another term coined by Whewell. In catastrophism, the earth and its inhabitants have been affected by short-lived violent events, such as volcanic eruptions and earthquakes. From the 1850s to the 1980s uniformitarianism was the dominant paradigm of geology. Then, on 6 June 1980, a paper was published in the highly respected journal *Science*. It proposed a catastrophic end to the reign of the dinosaurs. The paper was the result of the collaborative work of Luis Alvarez, a Nobel prize winning physicist, his son Walter Alvarez, a Professor of Geology and Frank Asaro and Helen Michel, environmental scientists, all of whom worked at the University of California at Berkeley (Alvarez et al., 1980). The paper, 13 pages long, presented a true hypothesis to the scientific community, not a theory, a principle or a law. Alvarez and his team presented their ideas with little concrete evidence to back up their conclusion, that an asteroid or large meteorite had impacted and that this was the final agent of the demise of the dinosaurs. From a How Science Works perspective, this hypothesis was actually the result of work to try and ascertain something else altogether – a different hypothesis.

The original intention of the team of scientists was not to find the cause for the extinction of the dinosaurs, but to find a way of calculating the rate of sedimentation in old rock sequences. Most techniques for doing this relied more on guesswork than a scientifically accurate way of measuring sedimentation. The problem with calculating rates of sedimentation is that it is never a constant. Very fine grained mud and the resultant mudstones may take centuries to accumulate in very slow moving or stagnant waters. Sandstones may be deposited as thick layers in a relatively short time, sometimes as the result of catastrophic events for example underwater sea floor avalanches, or sudden surface deposition of large volumes of volcanic ash, such as those deposited after the mount St Helen's volcanic eruption, which also took place in 1980. Alvarez and his team were looking for a better way of calculating the rate of sedimentation and hit on the idea of using a rare earth metal, iridium, to act as a chronometer for sedimentation.

Iridium is very scarce naturally. Although, when the earth formed 4.5 billion years ago, iridium was present, nearly all of this original iridium became concentrated in the earth's core. The iridium we find on the surface of the earth comes from an extraterrestrial source, meteorites, asteroids and the cosmic dust that rains down on us in minute, but detectable quantities. Alvarez and his team reasoned that if the rate of deposition of iridium was known, then, we could calculate the rate of deposition of sediments within which iridium (from cosmic dust) would be trapped. Their reasoning was sound; they had a testable idea – a hypothesis – which they set out to test in the field. To measure such small quantities of iridium, new machinery was needed. Being a physicist, Luis Alvarez designed a neutron activation machine that could precisely measure the amount of iridium in a rock sample. The level of precision was crucial, since measurements of the order of parts per billion are needed to make accurate estimations of the rate of sedimentation.

Walter Alvarez had been collecting rock samples (clays and limestone) from a site at Gubbio in Italy. These were used to test the newly constructed machine. The clays also marked a geological boundary that separated the Cretaceous era from the Tertiary known as the K-T boundary – the very boundary that marks the point of extinction of the dinosaurs from the geological record. Fossils of dinosaurs can be found in Cretaceous rocks, but not in any Tertiary rocks. The boundary had been dated as occurring 65 million years ago, the accepted age of the extinction of the dinosaurs. The clays at Gubbio were used not because they marked this boundary, but because they were thick – presenting good specimens for measuring the rate of sedimentation. Iridium is present naturally at an average of 0.3 parts per billion in rocks. When testing different types of rock the scientists expected to find variation: In rapidly deposited sediments a higher concentration and, in slowly deposited sediments, a much lower concentration. What they found in the clays at Gubbio surprised them. The average measurement of iridium concentration in the rocks surrounding the clays (limestone) was about 0.3 parts per billion. The clays themselves, however, had a much higher concentration of 9 parts per billion of iridium – 30 times what they expected to find. This spike needed careful interpretation. Having ascertained that their machinery and measurements were functioning correctly and were accurate, they needed to explain the spike. The simplest and probably an explanation that would have been accepted, was that the mudstones had taken 30 times longer to accumulate than the surrounding rocks of the same thickness, but with much lower iridium readings. They could have used this interpretation, written up their findings and put this into the scientific community with relative safety from being exposed as poor science or bad science. It did, after all, fit their original idea; they would just have to find an environmental reason why sedimentation was so much slower for this period of time at Gubbio. Instead the team looked at the results and turned the hypothesis on its head. They reasoned that an alternative explanation could be that an unusually large influx of iridium from outer space took place in a relatively short space of geological time. This new hypothesis needed to be tested and the results from their Gubbio samples cross checked. They looked for sites elsewhere in the world which marked the K-T boundary and which contained rocks similar to those found at Gubbio. Their reasoning being that similar findings would back their idea of a large influx, different findings of lower iridium concentrations would support the slow accumulation idea.

Rock samples from Stevns Klint in Denmark are crucial to this story. Rocks surrounding the clays there had readings of around 0.26 parts per billion – entirely consistent with the surrounding rocks at Gubbio and what they would have predicted from known concentrations of iridium. The boundary clays however showed a spike of 42 parts per billion some 160 times the expected concentration and much higher than those at Gubbio. They needed a mechanism for the introduction of such high quantities of iridium and the only plausible one was a direct influx in the shape of a large meteorite or asteroid. Using estimates of the effects of other explosive events, such as the eruption of Krakatoa (which incidentally is West, not East of Java as the 1969 film title, *Krakatoa, East of Java*, erroneously suggests), Alvarez and his team concluded that the iridium must have come from an extraterrestrial source and that source was an asteroid which they calculated to be some 10Km in diameter.

Since their paper was published – a paper that relied on very little evidence (samples from two clay outcrops) – there have been refutations of their ideas, but slowly, over the past 30 years, their ideas have been acknowledged as largely correct. The big question posed by the paper was could we find evidence of the crater that this 34 billion tonne, 10Km diameter asteroid left behind? The current contender and site of the impact is the Chicxulub crater, off the Yucatan peninsula, discovered by a Canadian geology graduate student, Alan Hildebrand. He looked at jumbled rock beds which were the result of giant tsunamis, around the time of the K-T boundary located on the coast of the Gulf of Mexico in Southern Mexico. This, coupled with concentration maps of the iridium in K-T boundary clays around the world, indicated that a crater must be present somewhere in the Gulf of Mexico. Boreholes and other geophysical evidence gathered in the 1960s by oil company surveys – which showed the presence of a roughly circular structure, showed the now identified Chicxulub crater to be where the geologists predicted it to be and to be of the size (150Km diameter) that Alvarez and his team predicted.

Crossing boundaries

There is more to this story than meets the eye from a How Science Works perspective. When the paper was originally published many geologists and palaeontologists rejected it – not surprising given how little evidence there was in favour of their ideas. More so, however, the paper was resented as it represented physicists entering the domain of geologists. Although one of the authors was a Professor of Geology – Walter Alvarez, the lead author was his father, Professor Luis Alvarez, physicist and Nobel prize winner. The other scientists were nuclear chemists. Prior to the asteroid extinction hypothesis, many other competing ideas for dinosaur extinction had been put forward, from an inability to copulate and effectively reproduce, to the rise of new plant species which inflicted major diarrhoea through a change in their available diet, to ideas that there was no mass extinction, they more or less gradually died out and fewer and fewer fossils are found until, at the K-T boundary they simply vanish. A similar, though earthly extinction hypothesis is that major volcanic eruptions occurred at the K-T boundary and these led to conditions similar to an asteroid impact which threw billions of tonnes of dust and ash into the atmosphere, blocking out sunlight and leading to the extinction of many photosynthesizing plants and subsequently denying herbivorous dinosaurs of their food, ultimately depriving the carnivores of their food source. These extinction hypotheses fell into two camps: a gradualist camp – where extinction took place over a very long period of time and the K-T boundary simply marks the end point of a natural decline and the catastrophists – who subscribed mainly to the major volcanic eruption idea. The asteroid extinction hypothesis fell into the latter camp. As such it made an enemy of the gradualists, friends of some of the catastrophists, but many of these preferred their volcanic catastrophe over an asteroid impact. At the hub of the dispute was the idea that a physicist should come into another scientific discipline and tell the community of geologists what to do. As the science writer Robert Jastrow observed,

> *Professor Alavrez was pulling rank on the palaeontologists. Physicists sometimes do that; they feel they have a monopoly on clear thinking. There is a power in their use of math and the precision of their measurements that transcends the power of the softer sciences*
>
> (Jastrow, 1983: 152)

The Alvarez team paper, when published, was given a prominent position in the Journal *Science* and it was featured in the general press as an important paper which explained, once and for all, the demise of the dinosaurs. In some ways it could be (and was) argued that the paper did not deserve such prominence given the lack of evidence for it. Despite its controversial history, the idea fulfils what we think of as good science – the idea was put forward as a hypothesis that could (and subsequently was) tested. The hypothesis would allow scientists to make predictions, many of which turned out to be more or less correct, the idea involved creativity and creative thinking – it utilized current knowledge and understanding to provide for explanations of natural phenomena. It is a good example of How Science and How Scientists Work. It is also an example of how science can be cross-disciplinary in nature. Although there may have been resentment of Alvarez the physicist putting forward ideas that solved a problem in palaeontology, subsequent to the publication of this paper there was a shift from a uniformitariantist view of geology to a neo-catastrophist view.

Physics

Pouring cold water on free energy for all

On 23 March 1989 two respectable scientists of repute announced that they had achieved nuclear fusion at room temperature in what was, in effect, no more than a glorified test tube. Martin Fleischmann (b. 1927) of the University of Southampton and Stanley Pons (b.1943) of the University of Utah published a paper in the *Journal of Electroanalytical Chemistry* (Fleischmann and Pons, 1989). On 11 March 1989 they had submitted a paper for publication and reviewed this on 22 March. On 23 March they went to the press to announce their discovery. The date of publication of the journal article was

24 March 1989. Their press conference, prior to actual publication, was an unorthodox way of releasing information about such an important and revolutionary discovery. Such a discovery would, if correct, have a major impact on society as a whole. The key to their discovery was the idea that the energy output from a fusion reaction in cold (room temperature) 'heavy water' was significantly greater than the energy input. Their experiment was deceptively simple. You take water that has a higher than normal proportion of the hydrogen isotope deuterium and you electrolyze it using a palladium electrode. In so doing, claimed Fleischmann and Pons, heat is generated that could only be explained by some form of nuclear fusion reaction occurring.

The Fleischmann and Pons announcement drew a lot of media attention. Subsequent to the publication of their paper, many laboratories across the United States and around the world attempted to repeat the experiments. A few initially reported success, but most failed to get the same results as Fleischmann and Pons. Even those who initially reported a successful outcome for their experiments had difficulty reproducing the Fleischmann and Pons results. For a number of weeks and months after the announcement, claims and counterclaims kept 'cold fusion' in the news. In July and November 1989, the science journal *Nature* published articles critical of cold fusion. Articles showing negative results in experiments designed to repeat the original experiment were also published in several scientific journals for example *Science* and *Physical Review Letters*.

The announcement by Fleischmann and Pons did attract some large investors who backed their discovery and wanted to exploit cold water fusion. In August 1989, for example, the state of Utah invested $4.5 million to create the National Cold Fusion Institute. In November 1989 the United States Department of Energy reviewed cold fusion theory and research and concluded there was no convincing evidence that useful sources of energy would result from 'cold fusion'. Between 1992 and 1997, Japan's Ministry of International Trade and Industry put millions of Dollars into cold fusion research, but ended their unsuccessful and unproductive research programme into cold fusion in 1997.

Cold fusion research is not dead, even today. Those who do accept the reality of cold fusion complain that they are unable to get research funding and that publication of their ideas is blocked by the scientific community, which has rejected the idea as having little to no credible evidence to back it up. In 1990 there was an international conference on cold fusion, subsequent to that conference, others have been held and in 2004 the International Society for Condensed Matter Nuclear Science (ISCMNS) was created. Occasionally cold fusion ideas still surface and papers, with the central idea of cold fusion are still published in conference proceedings. The story of cold water fusion again demonstrates key elements of the process of science – How Science Works and focuses on being able to repeat and replicate experiments – a characteristic of good science.

Chemistry
Phlogiston, or, how to ignite a row in chemistry
Chemists need to make accurate and precise measurements. While many talk about the 'bucket' chemist who just chucks in a dollop of chemical to their experiments, scientists working as chemists or in chemistry-related disciplines actually prefer specific amounts, often calculating these from their knowledge and understanding of the properties of the chemicals they are working with and researching. The man credited for bringing a sense of accuracy to the discipline of chemistry is the French scientist Antoine Laurent Lavoisier (1743–1794). He moved chemistry from an observational science to one where weighing and accurately measuring and recording the products, reagents and reactants became a standard practice in the chemistry laboratory. Lavoisier was a rich citizen, having inherited a fortune from his father. He was a member of the French aristocracy. As well as being a scientist he was also a private tax collector. This led ultimately to public execution on the Guillotine on the afternoon of his trial, having been found guilty of being a traitor, during the French Revolution. An appeal was immediately launched on the day of his trial once the verdict was announced. The appeal was to spare him from execution and allow him to carry on his scientific work, but this was rejected by the judge who deemed that the French Republic had no need for scientists (Duveen, 1954).

As well as making chemistry a more exact science, he also established, in scientific terms, the difference between elements and compounds. He is most famous for the discovery of oxygen – the story of which makes for an interesting case for How Science Works as it involves shared discovery with Joseph Priestley (1733–1804) the British chemist and Carl Wilhelm Scheele (1742–1786) the Swedish chemist. The discovery of the gaseous element oxygen disproved the prevailing idea of phlogiston.

Phlogiston, a mysterious substance, was proposed as early as the seventeenth century by Johann Joachim Becher (1635–1682) and Georg Ernst Stahl (1659–1734) as the substance which gave things the property of burning. During burning, this substance, phlogiston, was released. The resultant product, often called *calx,* was often described as a de-phlogisticated form of the original substance. The common observation in the seventeenth and early eighteenth centuries was that after burning the products weigh less than the original – the 'lost' substance, naturally, being phlogiston. It was Lavoisier who, in 1772, discovered that certain substances, for example sulphur and phosphorous, can gain mass when they are burned in air.

Joseph Priestley was a keen supporter of phlogiston theory and his experiments were not about refuting or falsifying accepted science. His work on the oxidization of mercury, its subsequent decomposition and release of a 'strange' gas that enabled things to burn more vigorously than in ordinary air, paradoxically, provided a nail in the coffin of phlogiston.

Carl Wilhelm Scheele first discovered oxygen in about 1772, pre-dating the discovery by Priestley and Lavoisier (1774). Priestley published the results of his experiments in 1775. Priestly met with Lavoisier in October 1774 and, in September 1774, Scheele wrote to Lavoisier about his experiments and results. Lavoisier later denied ever having received a letter from Scheele and claimed the discovery of oxygen (which he named) for himself, to the detriment of Scheele and Priestley. What Lavoisier did do was describe the process of combustion and the role that this newly discovered gas and element – oxygen – has in the process. He effectively disproved or falsified phlogiston theory. For How Science Works, this story captures a number of key elements such as experimentation, priority and publication.

Conclusion

How scientists work depends not just on the discipline within which they work, but also the type of scientist that they have developed into. Certain aspects of scientific work is a matter of routine – most scientists working today in research and especially in industry, follow set procedures and protocols. The history of science shows us that many discoveries are not a matter of protocol or working in a set way – not made by following a scientific method. Often, discoveries in science are serendipitous, from Priestley's heating of mercury to form mercuric oxide and its decomposition producing a gas that makes things burn more vigorously to Alvarez and his team, who just happened to test clays from the K-T boundary which showed huge spikes in the iridium concentration and the dogged determination of Lynn Margulis who proposed the idea of endosymbiosis to explain the evolution of the eukaryotic cell and her subsequent research to back up her ideas. Science also has dead ends. Cold fusion is a dead end. It may well have been proposed by respected, reputable scientists, but the evidence does not back up their claim.

The one common theme that runs through these stories in science is the role of evidence. Science is about the acceptance of evidence. The currency of science is data and data is evidence. Even if a scientist has a preference for a particular idea, for example Priestley, who was a robust defender of phlogiston, ultimately, it is the evidence not the belief of the scientist that should determine what is and what is not accepted by the scientific community as a whole. This is how Science Works and it is how scientists should work.

Reflective task

As a group, discuss any personal experience you have working as a scientist in research or in industry. Provide a brief case study if possible of your own experiences. Contact local employers/parents who are/were scientists and ask for brief resumes of their work as scientists.

Create (with the help of careers) lists of jobs that are science based. Then look at Chapter 6 Figure 6.2. And decide where to place the various scientists.

Classroom task

Your teacher will provide you with a figure (Chapter 6 Figure 6.2) that summarizes the different skills or knowledge that scientists use in their day-to-day work (e.g. investigate and experiment, argumentation, history of science). You may also be given a list of different types of scientists. Place the scientists where you think they belong in the different skill areas for example an industrial chemist will be almost all in the investigation and experimentation circle. Someone who works in medicine helping people conceive who are unable to have children may be in the experimentation circle and in the argumentation circle as they have to think about the moral and ethical impact of their work.

References

Alvarez, L. W., Alvarez, W., Asaro, F. and Michel, H. V. 1980. Extraterrestrial cause for the Cretaceous-Tertiary extinction. *Science,* 208, 1095–1108.

Brockman, J. 1996. *The Third Culture: Beyond the Scientific Revolution,* New York: Simon & Schuster.

Cresswell, J., Ikedo, M., Schleicher, A., Shewbridge, C. and Zoido, P. 2009. Top of the Class: High performers in Science in PISA 2006.

Duveen, D. I. 1954. Antoine Laurent Lavoisier and the French Revolution (I). *Journal of Chemical Education,* 31, 60.

Fleischmann, M. and Pons, S. 1989. Electrochemically induced nuclear fusion of deuterium. *Journal of Electroanalytical Chemistry,* 261, 301–308.

Haynes, R. D. 1994. *From Faust to Strangelove: Representations of the Scientist in Western Literature,* Baltimore: The Johns Hopkins University Press.

Jastrow, R. 1983. The dinosaur massacre: a double-barrelled mystery. *Science Digest.* Hearst Corporation.

Meredith, D. 2010a. *Explaining Research,* Oxford: Oxford University Press.

Meredith, D. 2010b. Scientists are heroes. *The Scientist.*

Sagan, L. 1967. On the origin of mitosing cells. *Journal of Theoretical Biology,* 14, 225–274, IN1–IN6.

Whewell, W. 1858. *Novum Organon Renovatum: Being the second part of the philosophy of the inductive sciences,* London: John W. Parker and Son.

Index

Page numbers in **bold** denote figures and tables.